YORK FILM NOTES

La Haine
(Hate)

Director
Mathieu Kassovitz

Note by Roy Stafford

Longman

York Press

York Press
322 Old Brompton Road, London SW5 9JH

Pearson Education Limited
Edinburgh Gate, Harlow, Essex CM20 2JE, United Kingdom
Associated companies, branches and representatives throughout
the world

First published 2000

ISBN 0-582-43194-8

Designed by Vicki Pacey
Phototypeset by Gem Graphics, Trenance, Mawgan Porth, Cornwall
Colour reproduction and film output by Spectrum Colour
Printed in Malaysia, KVP

contents

background   5

trailer	5	key players' biographies	7
reading la haine	6	director as auteur	10
social & political background	7	cinematic background	12

narrative & form   16

film narrative	16	other approaches	29
■ approaching narrative	16	■ todorov & equilibrium	29
plot & story	17	■ propp & fairy tales	30
■ which story?	17	■ genre	31
keys to narrative:		different readings of	
structure, time, character,		la haine	36
space, sound	18		

style   39

overall approach	39	■ the moving camera	48
camerawork	40	editing	49
■ deep focus/depth of field	41	sound	51
■ the switch	44	two examples in detail	53
■ distortion	46		

contexts   60

■ subtitling	60	influences	74
social & political issues		■ mean streets	74
in France	61	■ gangsters & the 'hood'	76
representations in la haine	69	■ American auteurs	77
■ race	69	■ America or France?	78
■ gender	70	production & distribution	79
■ the media	72	reception	80
■ US v. French culture	73	criticism	83

bibliography	87
cinematic terms	91
credits	94

acknowledgements

Thanks to Cathy Poole, Carrie Tarr and Tim Young for supplying materials and to the BFI Library for help in research for *La Haine*.

—///—

author of this note Roy Stafford is a freelance lecturer and writer of film studies with long experience of adult and further education. He is co-author with Gill Branston of *The Media Student's Book* (Routledge, 2nd edition, 1999) and publishes *In the Picture* magazine and an associated range of film and media studies materials for teachers and students.

background

trailer *p5*   reading La Haine *p6*   social & political background *p7*
key players' biographies *p7*   director as auteur *p10*
cinematic background *p12*

trailer

La Haine (*Hate* in the USA) was the second film to be directed by Mathieu Kassovitz and it catapulted him to stardom in France. He was twenty-seven when he received the Best Director Award at the Cannes Film Festival in 1995, followed by *Césars* for Editing and Best Film – a similar age to Orson Welles when he made *Citizen Kane* and Steven Spielberg when he made *Duel*. Comparisons with these two major directors did not seem unreasonable, given the impact of *La Haine*.

> The movie rocked me, I left my seat thinking, here is a young film-maker who finally has the maturity and depth to deal with urban unrest without losing his soul.
>
> *Jodie Foster, as reported on several websites,*
> *giving her reasons for distributing* La Haine *in the US*
> *through her company, Egg Productions*

> ... a film which impressed me more than any other – Mathieu Kassovitz's *La Haine* .... There are very few films that have left me speechless .... This film must be added to the list.
>
> *Susan Morrison,* cineACTION, *no.39, 1995*

> ... stunning camera-work, terrific editing (the dissolves from scene-to-scene are perfect) and a soundtrack which echoes the action memorably. If you feel put off by the b&w photography or documentary feel, don't be. You won't notice these aspects because they are fundamental to the film and only add to its intensity. That this film led to riots should be no surprise – you'll feel the same way afterwards! Watch it.
>
> *Damian Cannon,* Movie Reviews, *UK, 1997 (Internet site)*

Hate is more than an enraged indictment of urban savageries. It is an elegant and sophisticated film full of humour and irony captured within a decidedly tragic framework. And it introduces us to aspects of urban France not readily available in French films.

Kevin Elstob, Film Quarterly, *Winter 1997–8*

... a message picture, so hyper-realistic and visceral that the estate's claustrophobia and the no-hope scenario of its youthful population filter through like a scream.

George Bailey, Empire, *December 1995*

... a film that brings such a searing portrait of urban despair to the screen, joking nihilistically right up to its final Mexican stand-off.

Chris Darke, Sight and Sound, *November 1995*

As the quotes above indicate (and there are many more like this), *La Haine* is a powerful film, with an emotional impact derived from the story of twenty hours in the lives of three youths and the way that story is presented. It is this double attraction of an intelligent film with a message and an aesthetic that has earned it critical superlatives: its writer/director Mathieu Kassovitz is a 'talent to watch'. The film found small but enthusiastic audiences in Britain and North America following major success in France. It has been regularly screened over the last four years and looks set to be essential viewing for fans and academics alike.

reading la haine

La Haine is different from the majority of French films released in Britain and North America (although more like *La Haine* are beginning to appear). It offers a view of French life not often seen in Britain, but one that is relevant to all developed nations which have failed to solve the problems of unemployment, public housing, immigration and policing. It raises disturbing issues about who is to blame for not recognising the crisis in society and failing to develop solutions. It questions ideas of identity and hybridity – challenging the idea of 'assimilation'. To say it is a film rich in issues and questions is an understatement.

its love of cinema and its passion

The stylish use of camerawork, sound and editing in the film alongside the social commitment have prompted comparisons with a range of major film-makers – in particular Spike Lee and Martin Scorsese. Most of these comparisons are with US directors and Kassovitz's use of American, especially African–American, cultural signifiers to present his arguments is a major discussion point for critics. But *La Haine* is French in its love of cinema and its passion, with tremendous performances from its young cast. (See also Narrative & Form: Different readings of *La Haine*.)

social & political background

The story of *La Haine* is derived from a 'real life incident' when a youth was shot by police on a housing estate outside Paris. The film's central characters, Saïd, Vinz and Hubert, unemployed and dependent on petty crime and drug dealing, are representatives of a multiracial community on an estate which is viewed as alien by polite French society. The youths' journey to the city on the night after a shooting incident focuses attention on their isolation and social deprivation. Conflict with the police appears inevitable and the film challenges its audience to consider the consequences. The social and cultural context of the film is explored in detail in Contexts.

key players' biographies

MATHIEU KASSOVITZ

Mathieu Kassovitz, the director and screen writer, has the great advantage of parents from the film industry – his father as a director, his mother as an editor. Like two of the successful young directors of the 1980s, Luc Besson and Léos Carax, Kassovitz was able to make short films (*courts métrages*), before moving on to features. *Fierrot le pou* (wordplay on *Pierrot le fou*) (France, 1990) is about a white boy who wants to be a basketball star. This was followed by *Cauchemar blanc* (*White Nightmare*) (France, 1991) and *Assassins* (France, 1992). None of these was released in the UK.

His first feature, *Métisse* (France, 1993) is available on video in the US, where it is known as *Café Au Lait*. The title refers to a 'mixed race' person and the film tells the story of a girl who becomes pregnant, but does not know whether the father is her Jewish boyfriend (played by Kassovitz) or her African-French boyfriend (played by Hubert Koundé).

Kassovitz's first experience of cinema was as an actor and in 1994 he took the supporting role in *Regarde les hommes tomber* (*They All Fall Down*) directed by Jacques Audiard with Jean Louis Trintignant as lead. Kassovitz plays a young man with learning difficulties who becomes the criminal partner of a dissolute gambler. In 1996, after *La Haine*, the same team of Audiard, Kassovitz and Trintignant made *Self-Made Hero (Un héros très discret)* with Kassovitz as the main character. Following *La Haine* this was Kassovitz's second major success, in a film about the myth of French Resistance heroes in the Second World War. Audiard won the Cannes Script prize and Kassovitz was highly praised for his performance – he was deemed *l'enfant terrible* of French cinema after another combative display at Cannes. The film was successful as an arthouse release in the UK.

After the success of *La Haine*, Kassovitz was able to make a third feature, *Assassins* – a longer version of his early short – in 1997. This film 'took on' the media and its treatment of violence in much the same way as *La Haine* took on the police. However, this time the reception of the film at Cannes was terrible – the backlash against Kassovitz had begun – and the subsequent release in French cinemas was not successful As a result, the film was not picked up for distribution in the UK or the US.

Kassovitz has continued to act, in relatively small parts, for example, in *The Fifth Element* (France/US, 1998) and *Joan of Arc, the Messenger* (France/US, 1999), both for Luc Besson, and in *Jakob the Liar* (US/France, 1999), a Robin Williams vehicle directed by Peter Kassovitz (Mathieu's father).

In 1998 Mathieu Kassovitz joined Luc Besson and Jan Kounen (director of *Dobermann* – see below) to form a production company based in Hollywood to be called '1B2K'. This will develop English-language films 'outside the studio system' (reported by Canadian Broadcasting Company in November 1998). There have been many rumours of a new film to be directed by Kassovitz and produced by Jodie Foster, possibly in English, following Besson's success. For much of 1999 nothing had been confirmed apart from a title, *Déjà Vu*, and the suggestion that it would be some form of science fiction film. In November, *Screen International* listed a new Kassovitz film in its 'International Production' section, *Les rivières pourpres*, a 'period drama' starring Jean Reno and Vincent Cassel and produced by Légende Enterprises with Gaumont. This would appear to be an adaptation of a recent suspense novel by Jean-Christophe Grangé which won a literature prize in 1998.

VINCENT CASSEL

Like Kassovitz, his close friend, Vincent Cassel grew up within the film industry as the son of Jean-Pierre Cassel, a leading actor in the French cinema of the 1960s. Vincent first trained as a stage actor in New York and *Métisse* with Mathieu Kassovitz was his third feature. He has been the most successful member of the *La Haine* team since 1995, starring in 1996 in the popular Hitchcockian thriller *L'Appartement* and then in the violent gangster spoof *Dobermann*. In 1998 he appeared in the British film *Elizabeth*. He directed a short film in 1999 and is scheduled to appear in Kassovitz's next film (see above). Cassel is one of the leading young actors in France and his public profile rose in June 1999 when he married the Italian 'supermodel' Monica Bellucci, one of his co-stars in both *L'Appartement* and *Dobermann*.

SAÏD TAGHMAOUI

A friend of Vincent Cassel, Saïd Taghmaoui is Moroccan–French and *La Haine* was his first significant film appearance. Since the success of *La Haine* he has taken the supporting role opposite Kate Winslet in *Hideous Kinky* (UK, 1998) and played an Iraqi army officer in *Three Kings* (US, 1999) which stars George Clooney. He appears to have long-term prospects in international cinema.

HUBERT KOUNDÉ

Starring opposite Kassovitz in *Métisse* in his first film role, Hubert Koundé has not had the same kind of success in films since *La Haine* as that enjoyed by Vincent Cassel and Saïd Taghmaoui. He has been mainly seen in television productions in France.

PIERRE AÏM AND GEORGES DIANE

Two more friends of Kassovitz, Aïm and Diane have photographed all Kassovitz's features with Aïm as cinematographer and Diane as operator. They have also worked together on other features such as *Salut Cousin* (France, 1996), a comedy about an Algerian visiting his cousin in Paris.

director as auteur

It is perhaps inevitable that *La Haine* has been discussed primarily as a film created by Mathieu Kassovitz, who is seen as its 'author'. Kassovitz was indeed the writer of the screenplay and the director. He acted in the film and shared the editing duties. His contribution was such that it is not unreasonable to compare him with the novelist who is a sole 'author'. But Kassovitz was not the only creative force in making the film. The other actors and crew all played important roles and without them Kassovitz could have achieved little – cinema is an industrial production process requiring collective and collaborative work. Nevertheless, Kassovitz is seen as an auteur and *La Haine* has been analysed by many critics and theorists in relation to something known as 'auteur cinema'.

The practice of singling out the director as the most important individual creative input in the production of a film goes back to the 1920s. Stephen Crofts (1998) suggests that this early period was a form of 'proto-auteurism' and the directors who were singled out all had an unusual amount of creative freedom. Some of them, like D.W. Griffith and John Ford, gained some control over their own work in Hollywood, whilst others such as Sergei Eisenstein or Abel Gance worked in Europe where the tradition of film clubs and societies as well as specialist cinemas supported the practice of defining 'film artists' and discussing their work. Crofts sees this early period as a 'common sense transfer of the discourse of authorship from other artistic practices, epitomised in Alexandre Astruc's famous proclamation of the "camera pen" (1948)'. Astruc had argued that the film-maker could use a camera in the same way as a novelist used a pen. But it was rare for a director's name to help sell a commercial feature – Charles Chaplin, Alfred Hitchcock and Walt Disney were showmen as well as film-makers – and the Hollywood cinema of the studio period (1930–50), the dominant model of international cinema, promoted its stars and genres rather than its directors.

The further development of the idea of the auteur came in the early 1950s when young critics working on French film magazines like *Cahiers du cinéma* and *Positif* began to take the original idea of authorship and turn it into a polemic against one sort of cinema and in favour of another. The 'manifesto' of this critics' group has been taken to be a famous essay by François Truffaut published in 1954 as 'Une certaine tendance du cinéma'. Truffaut was then an 'angry young man' of twenty-two whose main aim was to vilify what he saw as the 'cinema of old men' who produced films in the 'tradition of quality'. These were films which were shot on carefully designed studio sets, following equally carefully written scripts performed by 'star' actors. The stories were conventional and were often based on literary or theatrical adaptations. French quality cinema in the late 1940s and early 1950s was similar in many ways to British and American production. Truffaut wanted to see something very different – a new cinema in which the director was king and in which the techniques of cinema, largely subsumed under the concept of mise-en-scène, could be used to express the director's personal vision (of the world and of cinema). The critical writing of Truffaut and his colleagues coalesced into *la politique des auteurs* which was mistranslated by the American critic Andrew Sarris to become 'auteur theory'. It was not a theory but a polemic – an argument that there should be films made by directors seeking to express themselves, rather than just 'telling stories'.

The *Cahiers'* critics spent the 1950s promoting their ideas of auteurs – some of the traditional European film artists then working, including Jean Renoir and Roberto Rossellini, plus an increasing number of Hollywood directors who merited the term auteur because of a consistent personal vision which was expressed through narrative themes and distinctive mise-en-scène. By the end of the decade the critics had begun to practise themselves and the 1960s' idea of an auteur was established

director as auteur background

the cinema was invented in France

through the work of Truffaut, Jean-Luc Godard, Jacques Rivette, Claude Chabrol etc.

In Britain the critical practice of textual analysis based on ideas of 'authorship' developed from the earlier work of the 1920s via Lindsay Anderson and *Sequence* magazine in the 1940s through to the writers on *Movie* in the 1960s. With similar developments in the United States, 'authorship' analysis was established as the dominant critical practice in newspaper and magazine reviewing during the 1960s and has remained influential for thirty years or more (viz. the numerous books and magazine articles based on the work of a single film director). In academic film studies, however, 'authorship' was soon under attack as being simplistic and untheorised. Film directors did not disappear as a focus for attention but the concept of authorship was subjected to severe interrogation and its centrality was displaced by attention to texts in context, intertextuality, audiences etc. in the decades of theoretical struggle which followed.

'Not only the author and the text but, just as importantly, the reading must be seen as historically and culturally shaped. Time and place will, almost always, divide the moment of production from the moment of reading. The "meaning" of any text will thus vary, as will that of any author-name which may be attached to it' (Crofts, 1998).

cinematic background
AUTEUR CINEMA IN FRANCE

Following Crofts (see Director as Auteur above), it is essential to place Mathieu Kassovitz in relation to the development of French cinema since the 1960s. Historically, although the cinema was invented in France and French film-makers have made important contributions to world cinema throughout its history, cinema audiences in France never reached the level of British attendances in the 1940s or American attendances at any time. Attendances in France remained relatively static during the 1950s and when the decline came in the 1960s it was much less dramatic than in Britain. In 1971 French attendances outstripped those in Britain for the first time and they have remained ahead ever since. Similarly, with the

director as auteur background

the cinema was invented in France

LA HAINE

number of films produced, France moved ahead of Britain in the 1960s (based on statistics presented in Vincendeau, ed., 1995).

France has consistently promoted the benefits of an indigenous non-English-language cinema as against the general proliferation of Hollywood film culture in Europe and, alongside Spanish-language and Indian cinema, also provides the possibility of resisting the hegemony of American cinema internationally. Whereas in Britain and Germany, countries of a similar size, American films can expect to take 85 per cent of the film market, in France this figure will be significantly lower, at around 65 per cent.

French film culture is different for a number of reasons. In industrial terms, there has not been in France the same tradition of an oligopoly of large companies which have controlled production, distribution and exhibition as in Britain and the US. Especially during the 1960s, there were many small production companies in France making only one or two films over a number of years. When the critics of *Cahiers* became directors, they often helped each other find investors and Truffaut was quickly able to set up his own production company, Les films du Carosse (named in honour of a Jean Renoir film). The practice of 'co-productions', involving production companies in more than one European country, developed in the 1920s and during the 1960s was the dominant form of French production. It remains important today, often now involving television interests in France, Germany and Italy. One advantage of the system is that without a single strong front office, creative freedom is more of a possibility for certain directors. Production of *La Haine* involved three main companies plus Kassovitz's own and two other participants. Although a completely 'French' production, the film was backed by the multinational television company Canal Plus and it also received support through the MEDIA programme of the European Union.

Support for film production from the European Union, as part of its audio-visual policy, as well as support from the French government itself, is important to French cinema. State support for French cinema dates back to the 1930s and takes a number of forms. One is the establishment of film schools. Another is a financial subsidy system. This comprises a levy on box-office receipts, the *soutien automatique*, which pays a small

more 'respectable' to go to the cinema in France

percentage back to French films and a second measure, *avance sur recettes,* which is effectively a loan to certain producers of 'quality films' on the basis of script approval by a special government commission (see Hayward, 1993). A further measure allows private investors to set up a financial group called a SOFICA – *Société pour le financement du cinéma et de l'audiovisuel* – which can receive tax benefits for investing in new films. Two such groups are listed as investing in *La Haine.*

As well as direct financial support various French governments have promoted cinema as an art form and as an important part of French culture, establishing education policies and regional policies to encourage cinema attendance outside the main urban areas. The urban-rural split and the heavy dominance of Paris and the big cities were main reasons why French audiences were not so large as those in Britain in the postwar period. However, the Paris bias and the general support for film culture amongst the middle classes were also reasons why the increasing levels of education in the 1960s benefited French cinema more than in Britain or the States. It is more 'respectable' to go to the cinema in France.

All these factors – the status of film culture, state subsidies (albeit at low levels), small production companies – helped to build an auteur cinema sector in France which has survived the 1960s and *la nouvelle vague.* Despite all the economic crises which have plagued the French industry, it has remained possible for a relatively large (by British or US standards) group of film-makers to continue to make low-budget films with an experimental or 'personal' feel. Each year there are likely to be some first-time film-makers and others who are well established but prefer the creative freedom of auteur cinema, such as André Techine. Mathieu Kassovitz was able to make short films and a low-budget first feature, as well as appearing in two auteur films for Jacques Audiard. But is *La Haine* an auteur film? (see below).

By the tenets of the 1950s auteur critics, Kassovitz certainly qualifies. Apart from his approach to film-making and his overall creative control, *La Haine* is full of references to other films (a sure sign of cinephilia), most of which are referenced in this book, and 'in jokes' about the crew. Kassovitz makes his appearance (like Hitchcock he appears in his own films). His father plays the gallery owner. His producer plays the 'taxi driver' (a double joke with its reference to Scorsese). At Astérix's apartment, the names of the occupants include 'Cassel' and 'Diane' (the camera operator). In Style there is discussion of Kassovitz's camera style, which, based on his own experience combined with what he has learned from his auteur heroes, helps make an authorial statement.

From a British and American perspective it is difficult to survey French cinema, as only a fraction of French production is distributed in English-speaking countries. We tend to see two types of French film: the relatively low-budget auteur film and the big budget 'heritage' pictures, such as *Cyrano de Bergerac* (France, 1990). We don't see some 'popular' French films which distributors feel will not travel (especially following the poor performance of the French box-office champion *Les Visiteurs* [France, 1993] in the UK). The film-maker who seems to defy all these categorisations is Luc Besson, recognised as an auteur in the 1980s as one of the directors associated with '*le cinéma du look*'. Besson, along with Jean-Jacques Beneix and Léos Carax formed a 'Second New Wave' of young film-makers who combined a fascination with cinema and a knowledge of other directors' work with a tendency towards extravagant visual style – '*le look*'. Besson was keen to make films about his interests in (American) popular culture, evident in *Subway* (France, 1985), *Nikita* (France, 1990) and *Léon* (France, 1994) which all draw on cinematic genres. The last of these was located in the US and made in English, establishing a new form of 'French super production'. Kassovitz has already made a link with Besson and the two are linked in the most recent study of French cinema published in Britain: 'a new type of *auteur* appeared, epitomised by Luc Besson and Kassovitz. Both developed an *auteur* persona but one based less on personal vision and more on high media profile, technical prowess and an address to a youth audience' (Hayward and Vincendeau, 2000).

It would be impossible to quibble with the comment about a high media profile, but this linkage does seem a little unfair in not recognising the social commitment which is present in *La Haine*. Mathieu Kassovitz may sit uneasily between different definitions of film-making, but he surely tries to maintain as much creative control over his work as possible.

narrative & form

film narrative *p16*   **plot & story** *p17*

keys to narrative: structure, time, character, space, sound *p18*

other approaches *p29*   **different readings of La Haine** *p36*

film narrative

La Haine is a one-off film – a generic hybrid with a strong authorial presence. The keys to an understanding of how it is constructed as a filmic narrative are provided by some of the decisions taken by Mathieu Kassovitz before the production began:

■ start from the ending

■ time constraint

■ a story rooted in reality

■ three youths as central characters – no single narrator

■ a journey to the city centre & back

■ location shooting

■ carefully prepared camera set-ups

■ lenses & filmstock

■ use of different forms of popular music & 'ambient' sound

Some of these decisions will be explored further in Style. First, we will consider some basic ideas about analysing narratives.

APPROACHING NARRATIVE

David Bordwell & Kristin Thompson suggest that a narrative is: 'a chain of events in cause-effect relationship occurring in time and space' (Bordwell & Thompson, 1986). A specific narrative structure is therefore a construction of events in a particular order with linking devices which tie together events separated by time and space. The manipulation of narrative, time and space and the deployment of various narrative devices comprise the main work of the film director as 'storyteller'.

Bordwell & Thompson also usefully distinguish between 'story' and 'plot'. A story will include all the 'inferred events' which aren't presented explicitly in a film, as well as all those that are. Inferred events could include the experiences of the characters as children or the readers' assumptions about what characters might be doing when they don't appear on screen, but are involved in the narrative. The 'plot' includes the same explicitly presented events plus all the non-diegetic information supplied by the film-maker. Diegesis refers to the presentation of the fictional world on the screen. Anything 'diegetic' belongs in the world of the film – characters could use it or experience it directly. Non-diegetic information might be the titles overlaid on the action. *La Haine* includes several such titles which remind the audience of the time of day. The other common non-diegetic material is music or unidentifiable voice-overs – the 'voice of God' – on the soundtrack. Essentially, what we see and hear on the screen is 'plot' – the sense we make of it is 'story'. The film-maker has taken the story and turned it into plot. The story, of course, is always bigger than the plot and because it requires audiences to play with inferences, it is also open to wide interpretation – different 'readings' of what it all means.

plot & story

From 10.38 a.m. one morning to 6.01 a.m. the next, three youths survey the aftermath of a riot on their estate, hang out with other youths and make two trips – to the hospital and to the city centre to meet a drug dealer. One of the youths is carrying a police revolver. In a final confrontation with the police, two shots are fired.

Put like this, the story which the audience might construct seems limited in potential, but the specific narrative structure and the way in which the narrative unfolds – the process of narration – are crucial in turning something seemingly mundane into ninety-five minutes of gripping narrative cinema.

WHICH STORY?

How much are audiences expected to infer, in order to discover the story of *La Haine*? How much is the story about the events of twenty hours in

'Atmosphere and title are what come first'

the lives of three young men and how much about the whole estate (and others like it) and the past twenty years of conflict between the residents and the police? There are plot clues to help answer these questions, but a significant amount of background knowledge about *les banlieues* is needed to get the full story (see Context).

In many fiction films, narrative questions or 'enigmas' are relatively straightforward: will the girl get the boy? will the murderer be caught? *La Haine* has such a central question: will the gun be used? will anyone be hurt? But it also has much bigger questions. The original title of the film was *Jusqu'ici tout va bien ...* (*So far everything is OK ...*). This refers to the story told at the beginning of the film (and twice more later on) about the man falling from the high building, who as he passes each floor on the way down says to himself, 'So far, so good'. The film's plot can be seen as one long fall. But in a metaphorical sense it could be the whole of French society that is falling (the third time the story is told 'society' is substituted for 'man'). The eventual title 'Hate' then refers to the destructive force which is destroying society. Seen in these terms, a narrative analysis takes on a very serious tone for discussion of what is a tale of despair, albeit filmed with an aesthetic which is vibrant and life affirming.

keys to narrative: structure, time, character, space, sound

START FROM THE ENDING

Mathieu Kassovitz has said that he knew the ending of *La Haine* before he knew the story: 'The atmosphere is what I am interested in describing, even before I know the story. This is the "message". Atmosphere and title are what come first. With *Métisse* and *La Haine*, I knew the ending before I knew the storyline. Everything is about the end, the last few seconds' (quoted in Bourguignon & Tobin, 1999). In a good interview Kassovitz goes on to argue that he is particularly interested in endings and that he believes they throw a whole new light on the rest of the story. This makes sense in recognising how tightly structured the film feels – that, although there is relatively little 'action' as such, there is still a strong sense of suspense.

TIME CONSTRAINT

The restriction to a tightly defined time period is unusual for an entire film narrative – often it is reserved for a specific suspense sequence. It is possibly a generic characteristic of some youth pictures, since youths are more likely to be 'out all night' and stranded by lack of resources, public transport etc. A twenty-hour period without sleep suggests an adventure, an uncommon experience. But most of all the concentration on a limited timespan helps to increase tension and to build suspense – that emotional involvement of an audience with screen events which creates the thrill of expectation of something about to happen. Suspense works by carefully feeding the audience with information, but always keeping something back. In *La Haine* the source of suspense is the gun and the condition of Abdel in hospital. If he dies, Vinz has vowed to kill a police officer.

The use of titles to tell the audience the time works in favour of the suspense narrative in a number of ways. How much longer will Vinz be able to maintain his self-control, before he does something stupid? How much longer will Abdel survive? The time passing also works symbolically. Vinz is like a time bomb, primed to go off. Each tick of the clock winds on the ratchet another notch. It is a reminder of the metaphor, 'so far, so good' – we are still falling, but perhaps getting nearer the ground. (Some critics, it should be noted, see the insertions of the precise time as having no real narrative relevance – Kassovitz himself suggests that they are there to refer to the television news and magazine programmes ('reality' programming), but he has also said that he took the sound of the ticking clock directly from a laserdisc of *The Hudsucker Proxy* (US, 1994) – implying that it was another aspect of his attempt to explore the use of sound.)

There are long periods in *La Haine* when 'nothing happens' – these are unemployed youths with nothing to do and time stretches before them.

the development of feeling towards the characters

The clock titles then emphasise the opposite pressure of time – how to fill the long hours of tedium. This is well illustrated in the scene where the younger boy tells the trio about things he has seen on television and again when they miss the last train. Their whole lives seem aimless and often the stories they tell have no real endings.

Overall, the manipulation of narrative time in *La Haine* creates a sense of unease – the ticking clock builds up tension which is exacerbated by the meanderings and frustration shown by the youths. By contrast, the opening montage of news footage of the riot emphasises the 'rush' of adrenaline created by the disturbance. The riot is something new and seemingly purposeful compared to the pointlessness of life on the estate.

The manipulation of time is limited to the credit sequence montage (which may refer to riots on the estates generally both 'now' and in the past, but is most likely to refer to the specific riot of the previous night). The only time when the trio is split up and the action may be in parallel time is when Saïd and Hubert are arrested and Vinz escapes to go to the cinema and a boxing match. Earlier in the opening part of the narrative, the action follows Vinz and Saïd and then Hubert separately, but we assume that the action is presented in sequence with compression of 'dead time' to bring it down to the ninety-five minutes of screen time. Here again, the clock prevents the audience from thinking that this is a conventional linear narrative:

> it enables the audience to understand that they are not following a linear plot, they are being presented with an event at a specific time: the hours go by and then something is going to happen at one precise moment. That's why the audience don't mind there being no plot, it's like a diary or a news report.
>
> *Mathieu Kassovitz, quoted in Bourguignon & Tobin, 1999*

There is a plot of course – in Bordwell & Thompson's terms. It is a very carefully constructed plot, but Kassovitz is trying to emphasise that the important issue for the audience is not the following of narrative action as such but the development of feeling towards the characters and their situation and the build-up of tension about what might happen.

A STORY ROOTED IN REALITY

In the introduction to the initial script and in the interviews in which he promoted the film, Kassovitz made reference to a real-life incident in which an eighteen-year-old black youth was shot dead by a police officer during interrogation in 1992. (McNeill [1998] refers to a sixteen-year-old Zaïrean in 1993 – one of the protester's placards in the opening montage of La Haine refers to 'Mako'.) The story of La Haine and specifically the 'spark' of the shooting of Abdel are thus rooted in the 'reality' of newspaper and other media reports. (Kassovitz and his friend Vincent Cassel did not live on the estates, but they were aware of the conflict with the police and had taken part in demonstrations – to this extent, their experience was 'first hand'.) As the debates around La Haine have revealed, there have been several other incidents in which black and Beur youths have been killed in conflicts with the police (see McNeill, 1998).

Vincent Cassel is quoted as saying, 'A kid got shot in the head in the eighteenth arrondissement, and maybe 500 people came to the demonstration in the street. Two million people came to see our movie. People might reproach us for doing a movie like this, but at least it's a step in the right direction' (Premiere (US), February 1996 – Kassovitz used the same quote in interviews elsewhere).

Kassovitz has said that he developed the idea from the starting point of 'a boy who wakes up one morning, not realising that this day will be his last' (Empire, November 1995). This sounds very much like the auteur explaining his motivation or the director pitching a story to a producer. Kassovitz does not mention him directly, but the producer/director who more than most took his stories from news reports was Sam Fuller, an ex-newspaper man and an innovator in the use of the camera. Fuller's low-budget work attracted many European fans amongst young directors in the 1960s and his films would provide a useful comparison for La Haine (in terms of camera style as well as narrative).

THREE YOUTHS AS CENTRAL CHARACTERS – NO SINGLE NARRATOR

La Haine is unusual in having three central protagonists. Hubert, Saïd and Vinz are perhaps unlikely 'mates'. Although they might all live on the same estate, their different ethnic backgrounds – West African-French, Beur and Jewish – would probably keep them apart. This suggests that audiences should think about them in metaphorical rather than realist terms (a point emphasised by the decision to keep the actors' first names and not to use family names – making the characters less 'real' in terms of 'documenting' a person). They are each 'introduced' by a visual device: Saïd sprays his name on the police van. Vinz wears his name as a knuckleduster and Hubert appears on a boxing poster. They are representative of oppressed groups in society and all three are part of a large single oppressed group – unemployed working-class young males on estates.

While they are 'representative', the three characters are also distinguished by different personal qualities. Hubert is seemingly the oldest (early twenties?) and most experienced. He is the most mature in terms of his relationships and level-headed in his actions. Clues scattered in the text suggest he has learned from his experiences – he was involved in serious criminal activity, but got out before he was caught. He has done service in the French Navy. Vinz is the most 'loutish', shooting off his mouth and seemingly on the edge of violence. He may be on the verge of schizophrenia (suggested by the hallucinations of the cow). Saïd appears to be the youngest. He displays naïveté and an adolescent wit backed up by a terrific talent for invective. But underneath he is pretty sensible. These personal qualities are confirmed by what we see of the characters in their home situations.

Hubert is presented as a young man with a strong sense of identity and an African heritage. In his room, as he divides up his hash to sell, we see posters on the wall showing Muhammad Ali in a boxing stance and the African-American athlete Tommie Smith giving the black power salute at the 1968 Mexico City Olympics. This last image is one of the most potent in the history of black culture – a defiant gesture of resistance to the American establishment as the American national anthem is played. The music he is playing is also American black music.

Vinz too is intrigued by American culture, but this time by the performance of Robert de Niro as the deranged Travis Bickle in *Taxi Driver*. We have an insight into Vinz's sense of identity with his dream about dancing to Jewish festival music. The dialogue in Vinz's home also emphasises his Jewishness. We never see Saïd at home, but perhaps this is because his is the dominant culture on the estate and he is more 'at home' out in the community, where his brother and sister are also to be found, in contrast with Vinz and Hubert's families who are seen only in their homes.

In one interview Mathieu Kassovitz suggested that his original intention was to make Hubert the character through whose eyes we see the story, on the grounds that he was the furthest removed from the action – it certainly couldn't be Vinz who was the narrator (Bourguignon & Tobin, 1999).

In the event, several sequences are 'told' by other characters because Hubert is not in the scene. Kassovitz is not a particularly reliable source, since it seems clear from the opening and closing of the film that Saïd is the main narrator of the events – his eyes open and close to signal the start and end of the film (but Hubert tells us the story of the falling man on the soundtrack in voice-over).

The performances of the three youths are strong – partly no doubt because to a certain extent the actors are 'playing themselves'. Vincent Cassel had more acting experience and would have used this in the creation of Vinz but Hubert Koundé who had appeared with Kassovitz himself in *Métisse*, and Saïd Taghmaoui, who was a friend of Cassel's with little previous professional experience, must have relied much more on their under-standing of the issues and their own 'life experiences'. (Kassovitz persuaded Cassel to shave his head and this helped get him into role.)

By selecting young men in this way, Kassovitz was consciously excluding older men – the 'first generation' of immigrants. There are no fathers in the film. We see Vinz's grandmother and aunt, Hubert's mother and sister (and we hear about his other brothers), Saïd's sister and older brother and the Jewish 'grandfather' figure who appears in the Paris public lavatory. Apart from 'Monsieur *Toilettes*' there is no parental/ patriarchal figure who tells the youths how to behave (but see below for surrogates). Whilst there are several younger women as relatives – all three youths have sisters – none of them has girlfriends. This is essentially a male and masculine text.

the most mature of the three youths

Hubert is presented as the most
mature of the three youths and
given some reflective close-ups

keys to narrative

The three characters have clearly defined roles. Hubert is the source of knowledge and experience. He knows his way round, he is accepted everywhere, yet he has to compromise. At the start of the film he has lost the gym he worked so hard to create (and he suspects that Vinz may be partly responsible). He must look after his mother, giving her his profits from dealing in order to pay the bills. Saïd is our guide through the more mundane scenes. He is curious and wants the standard experiences. He wants a girlfriend and excitement. He wants his just rewards from the drug dealer. Vinz is the source of danger and of threat. Seen in these terms, the ending of the film is desperate, as Vinz, realising how unhinged he has become, gives the gun to Hubert, the character in whom the audience probably has the most faith. Vinz is punished when he hasn't committed the crime.

A JOURNEY

Narratives which deal with journeys are usually concerned with the 'growth' of the characters, who learn from new experiences or who find themselves in conflicts created by the very different environments in which they find themselves. The journey in *La Haine* is short – about forty minutes by train into Paris – but it does take the youths to a distinctly different environment. This is ironically signalled by the poster which tells them 'The world is yours' (when it clearly isn't), by Saïd's first encounter with a policeman who is polite and calls him 'Sir' (which would never happen on the estate) and by the camera movement which 'makes strange' the image of the three youths against the Paris skyline. Later they try the old trick of switching off the lights on the Eiffel tower – but it doesn't work: they are tourists after all. They are not at home in the city centre and the journey enables them to learn something about themselves, but they must return, and by the end of the film they have not learned enough to save themselves. The journey also allows the audience to consider how isolated the communities in *les banlieues* are, compared to the city centre and how great is the disparity in wealth and amenities. Unlike some other films about *les banlieues*, *La Haine* has no scenes about the boundaries of the estate – one moment the youths are on the estate, then they are nearly in Paris. The estate, 'real' as it is, appears to be simply 'out there'.

an environment of open desolate spaces

LOCATION SHOOTING

The narrative 'space' of the film comprises the estate and selected areas of the city centre. The estate almost becomes another character. It is a soulless place, an environment of open desolate spaces dominated by looming blocks of flats. The camera is used to emphasise the 'canyons' between the blocks and the shouting up to Vinz's flat by Saïd emphasises the lack of privacy and of real communication between the residents. The environment brutalises the inhabitants and this point is nicely explored in the sequence where the television news crew attempt to interview the three youths when they are sitting in a children's play area. Hubert sends them packing with the explanation that the estate is not a safari park with animals on display – but for comfortable middle-class viewers it surely is something just as exotic. (The sequence is also playful in locating Hubert sitting at the end of a hippopotamus slide and in emphasising Vinz's ignorance of the safari park.)

Kassovitz's decision to base the shooting on one specific estate (La Noë in the 'new town' of Chanteloup-les-Vignes, north-west of Paris) and to spend a great deal of time setting up shots and getting to know the people on the estate is evident in the 'feel' of the locations as a 'real place', rather than one constructed solely through editing. Ginette Vincendeau points out that the estate chosen is not so obviously desolate as those with very high towers, but it is well known in Paris as a model estate built to house workers at a car factory that has since closed down. The problems of the unemployed on the estate are well known and the journalistic assumptions are accurately captured in the play area scene (Vincendeau, 2000).

CAMERA SET-UPS

Reviews of *La Haine* tend to overemphasise the use of 'documentary techniques' which suggests a narrative based on 'ordinary, everyday experience', like the 'day in a life' style of documentary. Instead, much of *La Haine* is constructed around a series of carefully choreographed set pieces which are rehearsed and photographed in long single takes. The long take here is less a marker for 'realism' and more an expressionistic device suited to a narrative which attempts to be a commentary on youth in the estates. Indeed, Bourguignon and Tobin refer to the film not as

reggae, rap, hip hop, funk, jazz, African ...

'realistic', but as a 'contemporary fairy tale'. This feeling for the more fantastical kind of story is created partly by the kind of camerawork in the scene where a local DJ mixes two records live from his flat as the camera glides out above the tower blocks.

LENSES & FILMSTOCK

Cinematography is also used as a form of narrative device. An attempt was made, although not completely followed through, to film the scenes on the estate with a short, 'wide' lens and the scenes in Paris with a longer lens (see Style). This has the effect of emphasising the closeness to the environment of the people on the estate and the relative distance from the environment – people stand out from the background – in the Paris scenes. Although barely perceptible in most scenes this has an almost subconscious effect on the audience.

The film is shot on black and white stock which suggests the downbeat nature of the estates, but also frames Paris in an unfamiliar guise (except for audiences old enough to remember the early films of Godard and Truffaut perhaps). The only splash of colour in the whole film is the Molotov cocktail falling to the ground in the opening frame – much more powerful because it is isolated in this way.

USE OF DIFFERENT FORMS OF POPULAR MUSIC & AMBIENT SOUND

There are several different ways to use music in a fiction film. It can be used to create mood and enhance suspense or fear or other emotions. It can be used to make a specific comment on a sequence or the actions of a character. It can carry a theme, repeating a specific motif. Or it can simply be used to enhance the marketing of the film by the use of a hit record or a performance by a specific artist. *La Haine* uses music to perform several of these functions but, arguably, it is also used in a more sophisticated way to complement the visual narrative in a coherent and continuous manner.

The use of different forms of popular music – reggae, rap, hip hop, funk, jazz, African etc. – and the choice of specific tracks suggests a rare sensibility and possibly an inspiration from other film-makers. Tarantino was a name mentioned by some of the reviewers but a more likely source

keys to narrative   narrative & form

is Martin Scorsese and his first commercial independent feature, *Mean Streets* (US, 1973) – very much a favourite of Mathieu Kassovitz. *Mean Streets* mixed black American music with opera, popular Italian songs and the Rolling Stones, both commenting on the action and developing ideas for the audience about the cultural milieu – using the music as a means of developing characters and moving the narrative forward.

It is difficult from an Anglo-American perspective to analyse the use of the specific tracks on the *La Haine* soundtrack, but the cultural diversity is evident. The film opens with the Wailers' 'Burnin' and Lootin'' from the 1973 album *Burnin'*. The use of this song from the early career of Bob Marley effectively links the actions of the youth on the estates to the universal movement of black people in their 'uprisings' against oppression in post-colonial Jamaica and in the racist societies of Britain and the United States. Although racism is not confronted directly in *La Haine*, this opening does suggest an outward-looking and universal resistance. Marley and the Wailers were still thought of as radical in 1973, not yet the 'sell-out' to the white music industry as seen by some parts of the black community in Britain at the end of the 1970s. While Marley himself was popular in France, his influence, especially in West Africa, saw reggae also entering France via French-speaking African performers.

But recognition of Marley on the soundtrack is more of a trigger for older audiences. The youth audience would be far more likely to respond to the rap acts such as Supreme NTM. According to one music fan in Australia:

> ... the DJ in the window is Cut Killer (a famous NOVA radio DJ,) and it's a song of his own mixing. I believe it includes some singing by a famous French singer from the 40s ('real' famous, but I forget the name), as well as a sample from Supreme NTM. There's also a loop that's the same one as used by Notorious Big in 'Things Done Changed' and the 'woop-woop' sound is KRS-1 (once again, I forget the song name!)
>
> *from an internet news group on the Acid Jazz Archive*

Vinz actually refers to the DJ as a 'killer'. The famous French singer is Edith Piaf (1915–63) and 'Je ne regrette rien' was one of her most famous songs.

Piaf (a stage name from Parisian slang for 'sparrow') literally grew up on the streets of Paris and became a massive international star. She sang romantic songs with great emotional power and remained true to her original fan base amongst the Parisian working class. The mix of the two songs (the refrain from Supreme NTM is 'Fuck the police') produces a powerful statement which manages to combine the working-class popular culture of Paris, a very 'French' culture, with the more internationalist and modern perspective of rap. Ginette Vincendeau (2000) also points out that Piaf was a heroine for the extreme right-wing paratroopers who fought against the Algerians in the war of independence, suggesting a very heady cocktail of allegiances in the mix. As the camera soars above the estate with its 1970s' apartment blocks and occasional tall trees, it suggests a notion of potential solidarity between generations and a general antagonism towards the metropolitan authorities.

other approaches

The keys above are based on what appear to have been Kassovitz's own approach to the narrative structure of *La Haine*. We can also explore what can be learned about *La Haine* as a narrative by applying some other standard approaches such as those associated with Todorov and Propp (See Branston & Stafford (1999) for more background on these two theorists).

TODOROV & EQUILIBRIUM

Tzvetan Todorov is credited with introducing the idea of narrative as a process of disruption and equilibrium. Every narrative is assumed to start with a range of potentially conflicting forces in some kind of balance or equilibrium. This is then disrupted by an event which creates actual conflict. The conflict develops up to a climactic point, after which there is some form of resolution and the establishment of a new equilibrium.

In *La Haine* the 'initial equilibrium' is the precarious balance between the anger of the youths and the repressive power of the police. The balance is only maintained through an element of self-control in each case. What then is the disruption? Is it the shooting of Abdel, the riot which ensues or the loss of the pistol which is found by Vinz? All these actions occur before the plot begins – this is often the case in film narratives. It does make a difference as to which of them is chosen as the disruption. It could be argued that because the important balance is between the police and the youths in general, the riot is the most significant. But for Hubert, Saïd and Vinz the pistol is more important. Is the film primarily about society in general, or is it the story of three youths?

The main part of the film is certainly concerned with the escalating conflict between the youths and the police, although for most of the time we only see the three friends, and their conflict is with a range of forces representing a threat to their safety, including Fascist skinheads and the angry middle-class residents of Astérix's block of flats, as well as the police in their different guises. There is clearly a climactic moment – the shooting of Vinz and the 'Mexican standoff' between Hubert and the police officer. Is there a resolution? No. We can only infer what happens when Saïd closes his eyes and the gun goes off. We fear that we have crash-landed after our fall from the fifty-storey building. This lack of traditional resolution – the 'open' ending – makes *La Haine* a progressive narrative in the sense that it draws back from a conservative resolution (i.e. one which neatly ties up the loose ends and suggests that the conflict can be contained). What might happen after the gun goes off? Will there be another, bigger riot? Will the authorities finally begin to do something about the underlying problems of racism and unemployment? Applying Todorov often makes the political questions about narratives more accessible through its emphasis on a 'balance of forces'. It foregrounds the inherent conservative nature of Hollywood films which conform to the 'happy ending' syndrome.

PROPP & FAIRY TALES

Propp's work on Russian folktales and his presentation of a series of common 'character functions' (Propp, 1968) is also useful in thinking about film narratives if it means that we can pose interesting critical questions about a specific text. *La Haine* has already been termed a 'fairy tale' (Bourguignon & Tobin, 1999), so applying Propp should produce some insights.

other approaches

The most important character functions in a Proppian analysis relate to the hero, the villain and the princess. The fairy tales Propp studied often concerned knights who set out to rescue damsels, who were 'in distress' because they had been kidnapped by an evil lord. The knight is sent out on the journey by the king, the keeper of order, and is aided by 'helpers' (e.g. a good wizard), but impeded by 'blockers'. The rescue of the princess is the 'goal' in the narrative and the new resolution is often the marriage of knight and princess after the villain has been defeated.

At first glance, the Proppian tale has little in common with *La Haine*. However, it is still useful to consider some of the character functions. The hero is perhaps a composite of the three youths. The quest is to secure the honour of the wounded Abdel (is he the princess?) – Vinz argues that shooting a police officer is the way to achieve this, but for Saïd and Hubert simply getting through the day in one piece would be an achievement. The villains are the plain-clothes police, especially 'Notre Dame'. The helpers are perhaps the DJ and the characters who tell the heroes stories and generally keep up their morale. The blockers are the other police units, Astérix and his neighbours, the skinheads etc. It isn't easy to see a king, a 'sender' for the mission. Perhaps the king is represented by the parents on the estate, such as Hubert's mother, who unwittingly send out the youths on their quest. Seen in this light, the gun is a kind of 'poisoned chalice' that acts like a temptation to the heroes. At the end of the tale, they appear to have resisted the temptation, only using it to fend off the skinheads. Abdel is dead, but his honour is still to be saved. But, in Proppian terms, the quest is never fulfilled, the villains are successful in stopping the quest. There is no happy ending, the forces of evil are too powerful.

GENRE

Is *La Haine* a generic narrative? What can we learn about its narrative by applying genre concepts as critical tools or comparing *La Haine* with other films from similar genres?

Although an interest in film genres can be traced back far into the history of cinema, the main interest in 'genre theory' only developed in the 1960s as part of the more general application of structuralist ideas. Structuralism can be seen as an attempt to consider the similarities of

other approaches   narrative & form

study objects – in this case film texts – and the ways in which they are constructed. Ideas about genre in film studies derive to a large extent from literature studies and the structuralist move to study film genres could be seen as an attempt to work against the then prevailing influence of literature on film – the concentration on the auteur, the single 'author' of the film, usually taken to be the director (see Background: The director as auteur). So, was Kassovitz creating from scratch or was he working with generic conventions?

The road movie

We've already noted that one of Kassovitz's decisions was to send the trio on a journey into Paris. Many of the narrative devices which propel them through their adventures in the big city are recognisable from American road movies. The appeal of the road movie as a genre comes from the conflicts which arise because of 'difference' – when the protagonists travel through communities with different values and beliefs. This can be represented as country v. town, sophisticated v. backwoods etc. or more directly in terms of race, wealth etc. A classic example of a youth-orientated road movie would be *Easy Rider* (US, 1969), in which two hippies ride through rural America on motorbikes, encountering ferocious opposition from communities who treat them as alien intruders.

There are other films which share a concern with youths from the suburbs experiencing the city centre, and a common device is to abandon the protagonists in the centre at night, exposing them to danger. A celebrated Hollywood example is *The Warriors* (US, 1979) which translates an ancient Greek story of warriors fighting their way home from overseas battles to the world of gang warfare in New York, where one gang must cross enemy territory in the city to get home to its 'patch'. The narrative of the road movie is often described as 'picaresque' – comprising a series of adventures for 'vagabond' characters. This loose structure does sometimes have a clear goal for the heroes and often implies a change in attitude brought about by experience. The initial narrative thrust of the road movie can be negative – the hero escapes from something bad, like the Joad family leaving their desolate farm in *The Grapes of Wrath* (US, 1940), or *Thelma and Louise* (US, 1991) on the run from the police. It can also be positive – a conscious attempt to go and look for a new life, a better life 'out there'. In most cases, however, characters are forced on to the road for a learning experience. In most cases, too, this eventually leads to a happy ending after obstacles have been overcome. In two of the examples celebrated above, *Easy Rider* and *Thelma and Louise*, the characters certainly learn a great deal both about themselves and about America, but the knowledge is arguably so dangerous that they must die. Perhaps this nihilistic sense of characters who learn but have no power to change their predicament is a key to *La Haine*?

■ Youth pictures

Perhaps the most useful genre definition to investigate is that of the youth picture. This is a broad classification that depends mainly on an obvious appeal to a youth audience – very roughly fourteen to twenty-five, the single most important age group in the cinema audience. In order to appeal to this group the film must also, to a certain extent, alienate an adult audience, and we have already noted that the youths are likely to be opposed to figures of authority.

La Haine is clearly identifiable as a youth picture – partly because of its adoption of the 'iconography of international youth culture', the largely US-inspired music, clothes and lifestyle concerns. The film is narrated by the three youths (one of whom is on screen or on the soundtrack throughout the entire film). They are relatively 'rounded' characters in the sense that we learn quite a lot about them. The other characters are seen through their eyes. This raises expectations that parents, police and other authority figures will be viewed as 'outside' the youth world and represented as sketches, drawn with little detail on the outline of familiar genre types. This is also going to be the case with other youths, shopkeepers etc.

Thinking about representations generally in the film, it is evident that the members of the youths' families are indeed built up by short scenes with brief snatches of dialogue conforming to the genre expectation, but also rooted in a sense of 'real' families. The younger sisters show only contempt or indifference towards their brothers. Saïd's elder brother takes on the father role. The mothers are long suffering etc. The characters the youths

Saïd is arrested at the hospital in
this classic image of 'rebellious youth'.
He is also the only one of the three
to be constrained by older male figures,
being rescued from this arrest by Samir

meet include generic types like the fence, the drug dealers on the estate, the TV crew, the boxing fans, the man who helps them when they try to steal a car etc. This is particularly true of the interrogation in the police station, where the evil cop tries to impress the more liberal one, who is disgusted by the brutality shown to Hubert and Saïd. The three 'extraordinary' characters (the boy who tells the story about the TV show, the old Jewish man, Astérix) all effectively 'put on a show', stopping the narrative. They seem much more part of the 'road movie', the string of adventures and strange encounters.

The one more sympathetic character, with whom the youths do interact, is Samir, the Beur police officer, who extricates the trio from the possibility of arrest at the hospital. Although his role is relatively small, the exchanges he has with Saïd and his brother, Nordine, are emotionally charged and crucial to the overall argument of the film. On the roof top Samir approaches Nordine, who denies he knows him, and when Samir rescues Saïd, he says: 'I did it for your brother'. Saïd eventually shakes his hand – to Vinz's disgust. We could read these exchanges as suggesting that Samir is the only rational character in the film – but that would be too easy. Samir offers to help Hubert with the gym, but Hubert turns him down: 'The kids want to hit more than punchbags now'. When Samir is attacked by Abdel's brother and a scuffle ensues, it is Hubert who helps Samir to try to pacify the youths. With Samir as surrogate father to all the youths, this could be a family melodrama (i.e. a genre more interested in the emotional relationships between family members than in action), but the sociological point is that no matter how many black and Beur police officers like Samir are recruited, the real problem is elsewhere (i.e. society's fall).

La Haine obviously has the potential to address a number of social issues or 'problems' – racism, youth unemployment, police brutality, housing and environmental/recreational provision etc., but it avoids the British approach of presenting arguments, looking directly for reasons and possible solutions. Instead, it emphasises a more French insistence on philosophical questions or a more American insistence on action.

■ The action/crime film

In Britain, youth has often been taken to present a 'social problem' in itself

La Haine 'plays' with generic elements

and, here, there are many British films which combine 'social problem' and 'youth picture' narratives. A common American practice is to make 'youth' versions of popular Hollywood genres. There have been 'young Westerns' such as *Young Guns* (US, 1988) and 'young action pictures' like *Top Gun* (US, 1986) – a high school picture with military technology. *La Haine* has been related to the 'young gangster/gang' pictures such as *Juice* (US, 1992), in which Black youth in the housing projects, drug dealing and rap music are all generic elements. The influence of the so-called 'hood' films on Kassovitz and *La Haine* is discussed in Contexts.

Mathieu Kassovitz names his influences as American cinema, but the 'independents' rather than the mainstream. We do not have to refer to his intentions as the basis for any genre study. There is evidence for at least some elements of all the genres mentioned here to be found in *La Haine*, but overall *La Haine* is not a genre movie, rather it 'plays' with generic elements in a post genre way.

different readings of la haine

Its 'open' narrative structure means that every audience is invited to take the narrative ingredients and write their own story according to the way they wish to read it. By contrast, many mainstream Hollywood movies are 'closed' – they present a resolution that leaves little space for the audience to do any more than tie up loose ends and accept the outcome.

Indications of different readings of *La Haine* are scattered throughout this book. Following Kassovitz's own statements, it has generally been assumed that *La Haine* is a 'political' film in the sense that it has something important to say and, despite its generic references and entertainment features, most readers will draw upon their own political ideas in deciding what sense to make of it. 'Political' here is taken to refer to politics in the widest sense of 'involvement in social and cultural relations' and there are many different stances which might be taken towards the film. We will consider just two readings.

different readings

The events of *La Haine* are rooted in reality – they could happen and they already have. The deaths of youths in these circumstances are senseless and most of us would want them to stop. Does the film suggest the reasons why the deaths happen? Does it suggest any means of stopping the next death? One reading might come at the film from a relatively detached viewpoint, seeing the problem of *les banlieues* as part of the general condition of the 'post-industrial' global economy with its underclass of the socially excluded – young unemployed men, fed a diet of debased culture and caught in a consumer trap of unfulfillable expectations of affluence. Their masculinity is as much a problem as their unemployed status, pushing them towards violent solutions because they have no alternative goals. The state is unable or unwilling to help them and becomes repressive in trying to contain their frustration. This reading puts emphasis on the global power of international capital and the consequent dominance of American culture with its detrimental effects on French society – importing violent behaviour. The solution is to change the youths' behaviour and bring them back into mainstream culture.

A slightly different reading might place more 'blame' on the French state and its treatment of the youths, based on racism and fear. This reading, whilst not denying the problems of masculinity, might show more interest in the youths themselves and the possibility of their redemption. It might be more optimistic in creating an anger against the actions of the police and recognising the adoption of some aspects of American culture as progressive, if it allows the youths to resist more effectively. If this reading is given slightly more support here, it is perhaps because of Kassovitz's own reference to the ending. When Hubert tells the story of the fall a third time he substitutes 'society' for 'man'. The open ending presents us with Vinz, who has learned a lesson and surrendered the gun to Hubert, being senselessly shot. Hubert, the reformed and more mature character is about to kill or be killed and Saïd – perhaps the representative of most of us in the audience – can't bear to watch.

Kassovitz's polemical outbursts in his interviews are sometimes misleading. He wants people to see his film and so he says provocative things (e.g. that it is an anti-police film). But closer examination reveals that he balances the police violence by showing the disgust of some police officers and the helplessness of others. He also shows the youths as aware of their own aimlessness and their need to change or get out (which Hubert articulates). The youths are not innocents, the police are not devils. *La Haine* is a complex text and deserves to be read carefully.

In Style we consider how these meanings are constructed via selected cinematic techniques and in Contexts how the context of the film might influence our readings as well as the ways in which meanings were offered to audiences for debate.

style

overall approach *p39* **camerawork** *p40* **editing** *p49*
sound *p51* **two examples in detail** *p53*

The success of *La Haine* is as much to do with its aesthetic as its content or narrative drive. Aesthetics are concerned with beauty and conceptions of art. The term is applicable to cinema when considering how film-makers conceive their films as art and how they organise the creative contributions of camera, lighting, production design, sound and music in production, and then editing in post-production, in order to present a coherent work. *La Haine* is notable for major contributions in all these areas. It is a film designed to be seen in cinemas on the biggest screen possible. If you have only watched it on video, you will not have experienced the full force of a film which for cinema audiences is an overwhelming experience – the complex camerawork and the subtle use of sound and music demand the big auditorium.

overall approach

La Haine is 'different' from both the mainstream of Hollywood film culture and from some of the more specialised forms of European or American independent cinema. Many American reviewers have taken the film to be directly influenced by the urban gangster or 'hood' films such as *New Jack City* (US, 1991) and have imagined that somehow it has a similar aesthetic. Others have assumed a social realist style associated with location shooting and a gritty content. More knowledgeable writers have noted Kassovitz's references to his mentors – a range of mostly American independents and Hollywood auteurs – and have recognised a whole-hearted commitment to the development of a suitable camera and editing style for this specific film.

The preparation certainly pays off in terms of the camerawork and then the possibilities for editing which the careful, choreographed shooting allows. A personal opinion might be that *La Haine* displays some of the best cinematography seen anywhere during the 1990s. It is highly stylised without drawing attention to its own devices, so that it registers as visually exciting, but not flashy. Overall, it creates a developing tension between a slow almost dreamlike wander about the environment, punctuated by sudden sharp bursts of action. This is achieved by the use of a highly mobile camera, often on tracks, and an editing motif which in the early part of the film always cuts on some form of 'explosive' image.

camerawork

Kassovitz worked very closely with his cinematographer, Pierre Aïm and his camera operator, Georges Diane. The crew worked on the estate for a month. They were conscious of not wanting to antagonise the residents and so the shooting was balanced between the need to prepare carefully for very complicated shots and the decision to take risks on shots which were unlikely to be repeatable. Kassovitz had a reasonable budget, but he was also working under restraints created by the relationship with the people of the estate:

> The aim was to make the estate seem beautiful, supple, fluid. I had the money I needed. It seemed too much at times, a bit of a come-on, like a pop promo when the director's ideas are bad. That's the danger – when you can afford to you're tempted to use every trick you can think of. That's the way I am. If I know I've got tracks in the truck, I can't just leave them there ...
>
> You have to know how to handle an estate, it only takes someone on the crew to hit a child because he's sick of being insulted and that's the end of the shoot. We all knew that. We were very tense, but it was good tension. We knew we were making a film that was 'different'. We tried things out. As a director, I refused to play safe and get lots of cover. I took risks. That was exciting. The cast and the crew did too.

Kassovitz interviewed by Bourguignon & Tobin, 1999

In the interview quoted above Kassovitz distinguishes between the role of the cinematographer to organise lighting and select stock, filters etc. and the camera operator who frames the shot. Framing is crucial in *La Haine*, especially in the way it is achieved by camera movement. Later we will consider a sequence in detail in terms of framing and movement. First it is necessary to discuss some of the techniques Kassovitz deploys.

DEEP FOCUS/DEPTH OF FIELD

The economy of shots in *La Haine* is organised around camera lenses so that, in the first half of the film on the estate, lenses are 'short/wide angle', but in Paris they are long/telephoto.

Lenses are measured in millimetres representing the distance between the lens and the image-capturing device – the film in a traditional camera or a light-sensing chip in a digital (video) camera. A 'short' lens of around 25mm on a film camera produces a 'wide angle' effect so that compared to normal human vision, objects appear further away but more of the scene can be 'crammed in'. A relatively short lens is useful when filming in enclosed spaces. A 'long' lens of 80mm has the opposite effect of 'foreshortening' – cutting out the dead ground between the viewer and a distant object so that it appears much closer. The long lens is often called a 'telephoto' – literally 'photographs across a long distance'. Long lenses are often used in films detailing outdoor action, such as Westerns or war films, allowing an audience to be taken into the midst of a battle or to see a group of mounted horsemen close up.

A photographic image is captured using a combination of lens and aperture – the small opening through which the light reflected on the scene reaches the film. The aperture is like the human iris. When there is plenty of light, the aperture can be closed down; when there is little light it must be opened. The smaller the aperture the longer the focal length and the greater the depth of focus – the portion of the scene in front of the camera which will appear in sharp focus. With a very small aperture it is possible to achieve 'deep focus' so that virtually everything in front of the camera is in focus, from objects a few feet away to buildings fifty yards away. This effect was achieved in early cinema where outdoor shooting in strong sunlight gave plenty of light for a small aperture. In a studio it was more difficult to achieve with artificial lights and so techniques developed to film the action in a restricted depth of focus – just in the middle ground, with no objects in the foreground and no discernible

camerawork

the depth of field is shallow

Vinz and Hubert argue in
the confines of a Paris public
toilet. The depth of field is
shallow and Saïd is out of
focus in the background

LA HAINE

style

camerawork

background to the shot. In modern cinema the shallow depth of focus is sometimes used in a scene to shift attention from one character to another – e.g. in a scene with two characters, one of whom is nearer the camera, the focus may switch between the characters as they speak – with sharp focus causing that character to stand out against a slightly fuzzy background. This effect is noticeable at the beginning of *La Haine* when we see Saïd for the first time. The camera suddenly moves behind him so that the back of his head almost fills the screen. Then it moves upwards and we are aware of a fuzzy background image with slight movements. As the focus switches, Saïd's head becomes an out-of-focus foreground and the background comes into focus to reveal the line of riot police.

Combining the effect of lens and aperture produces quite striking results. A wide-angle lens and a small aperture produce a very deep field of action, nearly all of which is in focus. This is the basis of the visual style of the scenes in *La Haine* set on the estate. A good example early in the film sees Vinz and Saïd walking through the estate on the way to the burned-out gym to meet Hubert. The long take begins with a low-angle shot, with the camera tilting down to normal eye level; Vinz and Saïd walk into the frame from behind the camera. They carry on walking ahead and the camera follows them a little way, but then stops by a petrol pump daubed with graffiti. Vinz and Saïd walk on into the background across an open space towards the gym, meeting two younger boys halfway, and then carrying on all the way to the doors of the gym. It is difficult to judge the distance but it must be thirty or forty metres. The whole scene is in focus, from the moment Vinz and Saïd pass the camera until the final moment when they reach the door of the gym. In the next scene, inside the gym, the camera moves constantly, again largely maintaining focus, but it is much more difficult inside the darkened gym to create the depth of focus with low light levels, so some blurring further away from the camera is inevitable.

The scene with the walk to the gym is unusual in mainstream features. Long shots are rare, unless they are used for dramatic moments (a sniper lining up a shot) or to emphasise a tiny human figure against the inhuman

the camera keeps its distance

scale of buildings or natural environments. This is not how they are used in *La Haine* – the characters seen within the desolate environment of the estate belong there. As well as the walk to the gym, there are other similar scenes in *La Haine*: the youths sitting in the children's play area when the television crew appears, the aerial shot with Cut Killer's rap mix; the youths sitting outside a shop as the boy tells the story about the Candid Camera television show; the youths walking through the estate and passing the police officers walking the other way. This last sequence ends with a very carefully composed image, as Hubert separates from the other two to meet a dope dealer. As he conducts business in the foreground, Saïd and Vinz are clearly visible in the background. Focus here is switched not by a change in the visual image, but by the mix of the voices on the soundtrack, which switches between Hubert and the dealer and Vinz and Saïd. In the shots where the camera is relatively static, it keeps its distance and simply records moments of inconsequential life on the estate. A similar use of the long shot is evident in Ken Loach's *Raining Stones* (UK, 1993), another film set largely on a housing estate (this time in North Manchester). This unobtrusive camera is almost documentary in style and much less expressive than the moving camera in *La Haine*.

The final sequence begins with another carefully composed depth shot. Vinz hands the gun to Hubert and we think that the tension has come to an end. The camera stays on Hubert, and Vinz and Saïd walk away, with Saïd telling another of his jokes. Although they walk right through to the next road, we can still see them clearly in focus when the police car pulls up. Now we have to race with Hubert to find out what is happening.

THE SWITCH

Precisely halfway through the film, the youths arrive in Paris, and Kassovitz plays his party-piece to signal the switch of location and change in style. Hubert closes his eyes on the train and when he opens them the three youths are lined up like a holiday trio against a balcony wall overlooking the city. What happens next is a trick usually attributed to Hitchcock, who used it in *Vertigo* (US, 1958), when James Stewart looks down the tower, and again in *Marnie* (US, 1964) when Tippi Hedren remembers her childhood trauma. The effect is extremely unsettling as the characters

The end of the 'switch shot',
with Paris now a blurry background

camerawork style

the Paris scenes are generally 'flatter'

appear to be moving one way while the earth is moving the other way. It is achieved by pulling the camera back on a track while at the same time zooming in. A zoom lens is, in effect, two lenses in a tube and the distance between them can be altered. At one setting, the focal length produces a wide-angle effect and, at the other extreme, is the telephoto. By pulling back and zooming in, the characters remain roughly the same size in the image, but the foreground and background are completely changed. Opening with a wide-angle lens quite close to the characters, the whole of Paris is in focus behind them and the foreground appears slightly deeper than in 'normal vision'. Zooming in brings the background closer but loses the focus and shrinks the foreground. As the camera pulls back, the 'foreshortening' effect increases (there is now more 'dead ground' between the camera and the subject). The characters in the shot appear to be in the same place, but now we tend to feel on top of them. It is difficult to describe this process and the best way to understand it is to try the trick yourself with a video camera.

After this 'switch', which is also marked by a sound change (to the roar of Paris traffic), the shooting is much more conventional for the Paris scenes. Sometimes the change is barely perceptible, but the Paris scenes are generally 'flatter' than those on the estate.

DISTORTION

One of the disadvantages of wide-angle lenses is that objects close to the camera can be distorted, appearing to expand to fill the screen. Faces in particular appear to loom into the camera. This is noticeable first when at the beginning of the film, Saïd enters Vinz's room. The low-angle shot shows a wakening Vinz looming into the camera, with Saïd clearly in focus in the background by the door. Towards the end of the film when Vinz fantasises about shooting the traffic cop, a rare wide-angle in the second half of the film emphasises the gun which fills the camera in a blurry outline. A distortion effect is also evident in the 'subjective' shot from the security camera at Astérix's apartment. This is a function of security cameras which must show as much as possible of the scene before them.

Distortion is evident
in this wide-angle shot.
Vinz is seen several times
as a threatening figure

THE MOVING CAMERA

Some of the scenes described above have used a relatively static camera. But the most striking visual feature of *La Haine* is the tracking camera which follows the youths as they move through the estate. This is the fluid camera of Scorsese and of the highly individual auteur of British youth-orientated film and television material, Alan Clarke (e.g. *Rita, Sue and Bob Too*, UK, 1986 – a comedy set on the estates of Bradford). Sometimes this camera follows at a discreet distance, occasionally it is 'in close' or performing exaggerated turns and twists.

A moving camera is usually found in conjunction with long takes. Action is organised so that the camera can follow what happens in a continuous take, without the need to 'cover' the shot from another angle. A long take might last twenty seconds or more. The actors' movements and those of the camera crew must be carefully marked out – almost choreographed like dance steps. It requires a brave director to shoot in long takes with no cover – there is only one shot for the editor (of course the shot can be repeated but that might lengthen the production time considerably). So, although the fluid camera might look almost ad-libbed, it actually requires very careful preparation.

Cameras are generally moved on tracks using a small trolley – thus 'tracking'. The trolley is also sometimes called a 'dolly', especially when it is being moved towards or away from the subject. Moving alongside actors as they walk is 'tracking' and also a 'travelling shot'. Moving in an arc in front of or behind the subject is 'arcing' or sometimes 'crabbing'. Tracks have to be laid and they can get in the way. On smooth surfaces (like a studio floor) a dolly could run just on wheels. Increasingly in contemporary cinema, directors use a Steadicam – a stabilising harness allowing a camera operator to move with a camera over uneven terrain and up and down stairs etc. Critics have generally assumed Kassovitz and Diane were using a Steadicam throughout, but in his interviews Kassovitz often talks about his love for tracks and the precision they give.

The moving camera gives the fluidity to the footage of the estate. Kassovitz uses a wide range of shots, but never in a way that breaks up the overall style. Some shots are memorable, but not disruptive, in proclaiming the cleverness of director and camera operator (this judgement is of course a matter of taste). Low angles from special tripods, high angles from miniature cranes blend in, but the extraordinary helicopter shot which accompanies the live mix by Cut Killer is simply a moment of joy – something so beautiful as it soars above the estate. This was a remote controlled device and actually malfunctioned at this point, as it was supposed to hover above the youths as they walked through the estate. Kassovitz left in the mistake and created a talking point.

editing

If the moving camera creates the fluidity, editing creates the tension. There are several ideas about the function of editing. It is *the* crucial stage in the narrative's construction. The story doesn't exist as a film until the editor begins to work. Two strong arguments exist as to how to proceed from this point onwards. Montage theories propose that meaning is created through the juxtaposition of sounds and images. This is editing which works partly by shock, as in the Soviet cinema of the 1920s. The credit sequence of *La Haine* is a classical montage of different shots of demonstrators, riot police and images of resistance cut to music. A rather different idea is that editing should be relatively invisible. Shots should be selected and transitions organised so that audiences can follow the story without noticing the changing shots – so-called 'continuity editing'. Of course, it is never so clear cut as this. Even within mainstream cinema, different genres have developed different traditions. We generally expect montage sequences in action films and more restrained cutting in dramas. Modern Hollywood in the era of 'post-MTV' film-making has generally moved to faster cutting to make a film feel more vital. Editing is very much about creating a rhythm, and in youth-orientated action films the rhythm is very fast – it is also often a question of cutting to music. Directors and editors who trained to make music videos have learned to cut to the beat. Conversely, European art films are expected to work more often with long takes and, by definition, use less cutting.

If you want to get a sense of different rhythms, try counting the shot transitions in a few minutes of a film on tape. Do this for several minutes

editing

at a time from different sections in the film. From this you can calculate an average shot Length or ASL. In modern cinema this is often down to only six or seven seconds. Even in the Hollywood studio period of the 1940s it might have been as low as ten or twelve seconds (Salt, 1992). Mathieu Kassovitz shares some ideas with both the long-take school and the MTV school (he has made music videos). It isn't surprising then to find both very long and quite short takes in *La Haine* (see the examples below). It is also noticeable that, in moving from one long-take sequence to another at the start of the film, Kassovitz uses an explosive cut. The standard convention for cutting, derived from Hollywood methods, is to cut between shots of different sizes or different content. The eye soon adjusts to a different image, but if the new image is too different, especially in shape or brightness, there will be a temporary disruption for the viewer. So, for instance, when Vinz does his Travis Bickle routine in front of the mirror, he ends with an imagined pistol shot into the mirror. We hear an explosion on the soundtrack and the screen changes to a blinding white light, only for the camera to tilt down and reveal the next sequence of Vinz and Saïd walking through the petrol station.

This technique is used several times and its effect is to punctuate the fluid movements of the camera with explosive transitions. This broken rhythm helps to build the tension of the day. A rather different effect is achieved by breaking the cutting convention, in the opposite way, with the so-called jump cut. This is when two shots are joined together which are very similar in subject and shot size. When one shot is replaced by the other, the subject appears to jump across the screen. This effect is used at least twice in *La Haine* as an economical way of showing the passage of time. In the first instance, Hubert is in his room and we see a succession of shots from a static camera: he is wrapping up blocks of hash, he's sleeping, he's smoking a joint. These are, technically, jump cuts (the convention suggests that the editor should 'cutaway' to a different angle between these shots) but they work well together. In the second instance, at the looted shopping centre, there is a breakdancing display and again the camera is static and the shots jump from one dancer to the next, all spinning on the same spot. Again, it works well with the music.

the film is created in the edit suite

There is nothing unusual about these jump cuts, but what is striking is the confidence with which Kassovitz selects shots for each scene. Occasionally he has to have a little joke (the Hitchcockian shot down the stairwell in Astérix's apartment), but most of the time he chooses the most appropriate shot and transition. To choose a transition whilst shooting is difficult. Some film-makers would argue that the film is created in the edit suite, where the order of shots may be altered. If this happens, planned transitions cannot be guaranteed. 'Shooting for editing' implies that the director already knows how the scene will be cut. In his interview with *Positif* Kassovitz states that the preparation work meant that no more than four takes of any single shot were necessary and that the rough cut came to 110 minutes. This was not a film that would produce a 'director's cut' with an extra half an hour. With the scenes in the Paris section there were structural problems in dealing with Vinz's separate adventures while Hubert and Saïd were in custody. In a sense it didn't matter in what order these sequences appeared:

> But I don't really like to discover this during the edit because there are always stylistic considerations that govern the passage from one scene to the next. For instance, when they arrive at the police station, on the estate, Vinz is in the back seat. He turns and that cuts in with him turning round inside the police station. Those kind of things are fun to identify, but if you don't know the order in which you are going to cut those scenes together, you can't use them.
>
> *Bourguignon & Tobin, 1999*

sound

Kassovitz has stressed in interviews the importance of sound in his films. Unfortunately, the main organising factor for the sound in *La Haine* is lost on mono VCRs. The film was planned so that the first section on the estate has a stereo track and the Paris section a mono track. The logic of this is to validate the estate as a 'real' environment in which the characters stand out against the background – in this case being placed within a broad sound stage. In Paris the background becomes less important and the

sound

style

layers of ambient sound

sound is also less distinct. The soundtrack thus parallels the attempt to use wide-angle and telephoto lenses.

Stereo means 'solid' and the use of stereo in the cinema allows a sound designer to compose a sound stage with real aural depth to match the depth of focus of the images. There are several noticeable effects in the opening half of the film. The atmosphere of the estate is built up using layers of 'ambient' or 'direct' sound: car traffic, train horns, dogs barking, people shouting, motorbikes etc. The sound echoes around the open spaces, reverberating on the hard walls of the apartment blocks. This is particularly effective in the opening sequence, when Saïd is shouting up to Vinz's sister high up in the block, and is himself being shouted down by an angry resident from the other side of the block. The voices echo across the open space, emphasising the lack of privacy and the disruption to everyone's 'quiet lives'.

These layers of ambient sound have a contradictory effect, suggesting that noise can be polluting and irritating, but also that a real community may exist – wonderfully captured in the sounds of Cut Killer floating over the estate (although the message is 'Fuck the Police', it is curiously soothing). All these effects work because of the way the camera shots have been selected. This is also evident in the two examples during the youths' passage through the estate, quoted above, when the sound focus is switched between figures in the foreground and the background.

Paris is presented without any special sense of sound – there is simply noise in the background and some snatches of music. This is alien territory where the youths are lost.

Music is used sparingly, which is perhaps surprising in a youth-orientated film which has spawned two tie-in CDs. As in the work of Martin Scorsese (see Contexts), Kassovitz tries to make all the music 'diegetic', apart from the Bob Marley song over the credits. Here is a listing of some of the other points at which music is used:

■ Jewish festival music, as Vinz dreams about dancing in the basement

■ Indecipherable music playing on a tape deck, on the roof during the sausage scene

- African music playing in the background, when Hubert arrives home
- American funk in Hubert's room, as he parcels up his hash
- Cut Killer playing Supreme NTM and Edith Piaf
- Hip-hop music, as youths breakdance in the shopping area
- Arab music, playing at the boxing match
- Rap music, playing in the car (Expression Direkt?)
- A brief snatch of dance music, coming from the door of the club
- Barely discernible music, playing in the art gallery
- Muzak, playing in the deserted shopping centre where the youths watch the news on a video wall

The overall effect is a documentary feel – the real 'sound of the suburbs' (although it has all been carefully chosen for effect). The music 'represents' the separate ethnicities and also mixes them to stress the developing hybrid culture. One of the tracks on the first tie-in CD (which includes music from *Métisse*) is 'La Peur du Métissage' (Fear of racial mixing).

two examples in detail

The two sequences below are taken from different sections of the film to illustrate the wide-angle/stereo and telephoto/mono styles. These are 'shot analyses', not extracts from the script (which was changed during shooting). They show the size of shot and the timing of transitions.

The first sequence from the estate footage begins with an 'explosive' edit – Vinz slaps the punchbag in the darkened gym and the cut is to a long shot between two apartment blocks:

```
12.42 LS through an alleyway between several tower
blocks. In the foreground, back to us and walking
away are three CRS police officers. In the far
background are V, H and S, coming round a corner.

     V: We jeered at the cops and spat on them, but
     they didn't budge. Then the jerks stepped
     aside to make a path.
```

two examples in detail style

Mohamed with a new exhaust

(There is also the sound of voices on the police radio.)

The police officers have now reached the oncoming trio, who turn screen right. The camera tracks with them. Vinz is walking backwards, talking to the other two, looking towards the camera.

>V: They were plain clothes men with axes. They hit little JB really hard. The third time, we laid into them. I swear I smashed one of the bastards.

They halt and all listen to the sound of a motor bike. The camera executes a 180° turn and settles on Saïd.

>S: That's a Yamaha.

Camera to Vinz.

>V: Your mum on a bike, more like.

Camera to Hubert.

>H: No, it's Mohamed with a new exhaust.

They start walking again.

>S: No, It's Vinz's mum on a Yamaha.

>V: Which Mohamed? Farida's brother?

>S: The girl with the driving licence?

>H: No, the one from the market.

>S and V: Ahh.

The camera is tracking them as they walk swiftly through the estate.

>V: Anyway, you should have been there. It was amazing.

They wave to some other lads.

>S: Tear gas and two days of being beaten up at the police station ... then back home to face the music at home I don't see the point.

> V: Get off my back. It was war against the pigs, live and in colour.
>
> H: I'd planned to get some dough and your stupid riot screwed it up.

Hubert comes on into the foreground where he meets and shakes hands with another man. V and S stay in the background, but it is V and S we hear high in the mix.

> V: I'll always fight for a brother.
>
> S: A brother. Who is this guy? Why get hit for a wanker you don't know?

H and the man exchange money and H walks back to the other two.

> H: Let's go.
>
> S: I mean it. Abdel's a wanker.
>
> V: OK but I'm not faster than a bullet.

All three disappear into a building.

14.30 High-angle MLS of an opening to the roof, S emerges. The camera follows him as he moves across the roof to where sausages are being grilled. Music plays on a tape deck.

> Sausage man: Hands off the *merguez*. Who's paying?
>
> V: Come off it.
>
> Man: Saïd, watch it, I'm warning you. It's five francs for everyone, except Hubert — he lives in this block.
>
> V: Five francs for one sausage?
>
> Man: No, for two.

H takes a sausage.

> H: Try one (to the others).

> V: I've five francs for me.

Camera 'crabs' round as H moves around S.

> S: OK, I won't forget this.

> V: Go ahead, don't ever forget.

> S (to man): Don't be a jerk, I'll pay later.

> Man: How? With your sister?

> S: Leave her out of this (spins round, clutching head).

> Man: Stop acting the pseudo Arab.

S grabs a sausage and runs.

> Man: Give it back you bastard.

S runs round a seated group, including his brother Nordine, chased by the man.

15.28 MLS A youth approaches the seated V and H.

> Youth: Got two francs?

Camera pans to two-shot of V and H.

> V and H: No, we're broke.

> Youth: Just two francs.

> V (to H): The judge gave me a month in the nick or stuff for the council.

> H: Community Service. That's shite.

> V: You've done it? The nick's bad enough.

> H: You'd rather do time?

15:49 MLS of S, his brother (N) and sausage man.

> Sausage man: He stole a sausage.

> N: I'll pay.

> S (to man): You're a liar, your nose is growing.

```
Sausage man: Watch out or I'll smash yours.

N (to S): Now scram!

Camera circles following S who moves to another
group of youths

(the shot ends at 16:53 after Saïd has discussed
guns with a group of youths).
```

What is extraordinary about this sequence is that the camera moves to reframe relatively complex actions – characters moving and speaking. The conventional way to shoot this would be with a series of tightly framed shots lasting only a few seconds each. In this sequence there are just four shots in four minutes of screen time and the moving camera has brought the action through the estate and on to the roof, whilst negotiating several meetings and exchanges. The camera is constantly reframing the action, but the relative wide angle and small aperture produces the depth of field which ensures sharp focus throughout. The shots are designated here as mostly MLS (medium long shot). As a rough rule of thumb, a long shot will enable the whole body of the subject to be seen. In a medium long shot, the subject is shown from roughly the knees upwards. Similar divides cover the medium shot, medium close-up (MCU), close-up and big close-up (only part of the face). The coverage of the estate is mostly in LS and MLS. In Paris there are close-ups (e.g. Hubert on the train).

The second example is from the scene in the art gallery, which in some ways is a direct echo of the scene on the roof – Saïd is again the catalyst for action in the social gathering, and Hubert is again the more experienced operator. This time, however, the youths are in an alien environment.

```
1.11.51 MCU of Saïd staring into the camera, Vinz
and Hubert in the background.

        S: It's awful, awful, awful.

S turns away and V comes forward.

        V: (Turning to H) Is that artist famous?
```

the black one's a real beauty

1.12.06 MCU of child's toy attached to the wall. The Gallery Patron passes in front of the camera, looking at Vinz.

> H: He will be when he is eighteen.

1.12.10 MCU of Vinz who moves in closer to the camera and then backs away.

1.12.24 MLS of the three youths at a long table with food and drink.

> S: Champagne, Martini, Brocardi. I don't drink that stuff
>
> H: It's Bacardi.
>
> S: I want some peanuts.

A waiter approaches with a tray of drinks, S takes a glass.

> S: Merçi, Charles.
>
> H and V together: Hey Charles, Charles.

1.12.43 MS Vinz and Saïd are sitting on the stairs.

> V: Calm down, you're such a pain.

Two young women come down the stairs into the gallery, the camera pans right to reveal Hubert who is lounging on the bottom step.

> S: Get that — real women! The black one's a real beauty.

1.13.00 LS of the three youths across the gallery. Other patrons (slightly out of focus) are standing or moving across the foreground.

> S (to H): Do me a favour, I want to talk to them.

two examples in detail

For the second half of the film, Kassovitz said that he wanted to use a longer lens and to have simple set-ups, utilising only a tripod and no tracks or dollies (although there is some hand-held work). In this indoor scene, the use of the long lens is not so noticeable, although there is a slight blurring as characters and objects get too close to the camera. The long-take strategy has not been completely abandoned in this scene. The shots detailed here range from four seconds to nineteen seconds, but they are achieved with a static camera and limited movements by the characters. Where the moving camera could reframe and 'follow' the action, the static camera in the relatively confined space forces a cut. This also leads to more use of MCUs to achieve a clear framing.

There has not been time in this project to produce and analyse a complete shot breakdown of the whole ninety-five minutes of *La Haine*, but Kassovitz's proclaimed strategy does seem to have been applied. As he states (Bourguignon & Tobin, 1999), the effect is sometimes imperceptible, There are long shots, long takes and wide angles in the second half of the film, but they are isolated cases – nothing matches the long travelling shots and compositions in depth of the first half. Only through repeated viewings of specific scenes do the care and preparation in camerawork reveal themselves. One of the great virtues of the film is the coherence of its visual (and aural) style.

contexts

social & political issues in France *p61*   representations in La Haine *p69*

influences *p74*   production & distribution *p79*

reception *p80*   criticism *p83*

SUBTITLING

The reference print for this book was screened by BBC2 in 1997 with subtitles written for a British audience. Specific French cultural references are largely left intact and translations of dialogue sensitively handled. The video release by Metro Tartan and some (all?) of the 35mm cinema release prints use American subtitles that are markedly different. Specific references to French culture are Americanised so that the drug dealer Astérix is renamed 'Snoopy' and references to money in French francs are converted to US dollars. This is sometimes annoying but occasionally helpful as when the fence on the estate is renamed 'Wal-Mart'. Most British audiences will know this refers to a supermarket chain, whereas the French chain 'Darty', the name referred to on the soundtrack, will mean little. More seriously, the American subtitles translate most of the youth's dialogue into the 'homeboy' language lifted straight from American 'hood' films. There is certainly a need to indicate the kind of language used by the youths but the effect of these subtitles is overwhelming. The intention was clearly to make the film more accessible to American youth audiences (although since the audience for a subtitled film is already self-selecting, it seems a futile gesture).

The best contextual reading of the film will be available to French speakers, although even they will find some of the slang difficult to penetrate (see below). Otherwise, British readers are recommended to seek out the BBC version (at the time of writing the film is also scheduled for Channel 4's Film Four pay channel – state of subtitling unknown). American readers will need to pick up on some of the language references below.

social & political issues in france

LES BANLIEUES

Les banlieues once meant simply 'outskirts', but has taken on a modern meaning of 'suburbs', too. To describe housing estates, such as those shown in this film, as suburbs might suggest relatively comfortable residential areas on the edges of cities, characterised by private homes with gardens. *Les banlieues* are indeed on the perimeter of the city, but resemble much more the high-rise estates of British cities or 'housing projects' in the US. These areas of poorer housing, usually in the public housing sector, are designated as 'inner city', but *les banlieues* are further out (twenty miles or more) and, as such, more 'removed' from the centre – this distance being emphasised several times in *La Haine*. Distance here is a function of town planning and good transport, but it is also a comment on the desire of the Parisian ruling class to keep 'undesirables' as far away as possible – expressing the acceptance of anti-immigrant and racist views by the city authorities. Despite being outside the city, it is possible to consider *les banlieues* (also referred to as *cités*) as a French counterpart to the ghettos of North American cities. They would appear to share the worst attributes of British inner-city estates and 'new towns' (built as overflow or 'dormitory' settlements) – poor housing and no amenities.

The French estates are not necessarily 'poor' in terms of building quality or architectural design, but like estates in Britain they have been perceived as such – i.e., as unsuitable or 'unfit for purpose' by the people who live in them rather than by those who planned and built them. The cultural objectives of the planners are mocked at the end of *La Haine* when the shoot-out takes place beneath murals of famous French poets such as Charles Baudelaire and Arthur Rimbaud – poetic 'rebels' from an earlier generation.

Les banlieues are large self-contained communities with few amenities or employment opportunities. The 'new town' chosen for the shooting of

La Haine has an official population of 10,000 (but is likely to be much higher if 'undocumented' residents are included) made up of sixty different nationalities or ethnicities (James, 1997). The increase in overt racism in France in the 1980s saw *les banlieues,* where most of the immigrant and second generation families had been housed, stereotyped as the site of urban deprivation, crime, drug use etc. The communities became stigmatised and presented by the mainstream media as alien – the location of the 'other', the hysterical definition of what is 'not us', 'not French'. Stories about *les banlieues* became stories about negative definitions of 'Frenchness'.

CULTURAL DIVERSITY & ASSIMILATION

Like Britain, France was a major colonial power in the nineteenth and twentieth centuries and the period since 1945 has seen France mirror the British experience in relinquishing colonial power while accepting large-scale immigration of former colonial subjects – often on the basis of satisfying demand for labour during the period up to 1975.

Although similar to the British experience, the history of decolonisation and immigration in France also reveals differences. The most important areas for French settlement abroad were in North Africa, particularly Algeria. The struggle for Algerian independence in the 1950s was long and damaging for French social relations, producing both a legacy of oppression remembered by Arabs and Berbers and an angry and hostile settler community who 'returned' to France after Algerian Independence in 1962. North Africa is relatively close to Mediterranean France, and many Algerians, Moroccans and Tunisians went to France to work during the 1960s (and, just as in the UK, second and third generations of these immigrant families are now part of French society).

The French colonies in Africa, the Caribbean and Indo-China were not ruled from Paris in the same manner as British colonies from London, and when independence was gained, the ex-colonies remained in much closer contact with French culture. France still has colonies like Martinique in the West Indies and they are recognised as part of metropolitan France, able to send representatives to the French Assembly. By staying in the French-speaking partnership, the ex-colonies in Africa, like Senegal, remain

social & political issues

tied to French currency and French customs as well as French culture in terms of cinema, literature, music etc. One consequence of this is that Paris, because of its industrial infrastructure and 'mix' of people, has become the single most important centre for African music and cinema.

This history has led to a French policy of 'assimilation' – everyone becomes a French citizen and part of French culture. This is contrary to the American sense of 'hyphenates' such as 'Italian-American' which imply a combination of distinct cultures. The power of the French approach is such that in Mauritius, a country which was, until independence in the 1960s, a British colony taken from the French at the start of the nineteenth century, the modern language is still predominantly French or Creole (a language derived from French and local languages), food is French and books and the cinema come directly from France. However, in contemporary France itself, the Muslim North and West African community has to a certain extent resisted 'assimilation', and this clash with the assimilationist authorities underlies much of the tension in *La Haine*.

RESISTANCE THROUGH LANGUAGE

Language is one of the traditional battlegrounds between the dominant and subordinate cultures in any society. In Britain this is evident in terms of class, region and ethnicity. The authority of metropolitan government can be resisted by refusing to use its language and, instead, claiming rights for completely separate languages such as Welsh or Gaelic, or through use of regional dialects. In the US, arguments over the use of Spanish create similar conflicts. On one level this resistance can take a 'legitimate' course – arguing for dual language road signs and dual language teaching in schools. But it can also be developed in a more provocative way by youths who use dialect or invented language (like Cockney rhyming slang) both to confuse and annoy the agents of authority. Use of language in this way also helps to unite the users in a common bond against their oppressors.

The development of Creole languages in the colonial empires of European powers in the Americas and elsewhere is a good example of the oppressed

'Creolisation' ... now seen as a positive force

people (the 'colonised') finding a way to live with the colonisers without losing a sense of identity. The colonised took the language of power – English, French or Spanish – and transformed it into something else: a new language which showed its roots but now 'belonged' to a different group. 'Creole' refers to any combination of European and 'native' – the term also applies to food and to ethnicity. The process of 'Creolisation' is now seen as a positive cultural force (see Shohat & Stam, 1994). The colonisers fought back by insisting that education and administration in their colonies used the 'proper' colonial language, thus creating class divisions between those who learned the colonisers' language and the poorer people who spoke their native language or some form of Creole. When mass migration to Western Europe began, especially from the Caribbean, the new immigrants found themselves in a much weaker position – having to use the language of the ex-colonial power to a greater extent.

The 'second-generation' youth of these communities began to resist the racism of the British authorities in the 1980s, and it is noticeable that one of the ways they did so was through the use of Jamaican patois, which was further circulated through the success of 'roots reggae' music – the 'tougher' and more authentic style of the then current popular Jamaican music – and 'dub' poetry, such as in the work of Linton Kwesi Johnson. The contemporary form of this language development is in relation to rap and, before that, hip-hop. British popular culture has a long history of being reinvigorated by the input of performers and styles associated with black culture which can be traced back to African roots and the history of the slave trade. More recently it has become evident that the long association with Arab and Indian cultures is having a similar influence.

All these developments in Britain are mirrored to a certain extent in France, although it is noticeable that attitudes towards the 'colonial' language were, and to a certain extent still are, rather different. English is by its very nature, an 'open' language, accepting words, phrases and even sentence structures from other languages and melding them into the main language. Arguably this gives the language a flexibility which enables it to respond to new challenges. But it also means that 'English' in different parts of the world has developed separately. There is no 'controlling body' for English. By contrast, the teaching of French in the French colonial empire was pursued with greater vigour, and much more importance was given to maintaining the purity of the language of metropolitan France. There is less acceptance of 'other French' than there is of the 'other English'. This, of course, means that the use of other forms of French, especially within France itself, has great power, as in *La Haine*.

Verlan is a form of Parisian slang, something akin to Cockney in London. Some words are spoken backwards to confuse outsiders and it is from this 'backslang' that the term 'Beur' is said to derive – as a version of 'Arabe' (see Tarr, 1993). The first use seems to have been in the early 1980s to describe the so-called 'second generation' of immigrant families from the Maghreb (Algeria, Tunisia and Morocco). Beur youth, represented in *La Haine* by Saïd, see themselves as positioned between the culture of their parents, who still identify themselves as Algerian, Tunisian or Moroccan, and the 'host' French community. In *La Haine*, the use of *verlan* is extended to include some of the phrases developed within French hip-hop culture. The process by which African-French rap artists can take language already worked up by African-Americans and reinvigorate it with both French and African words and then mix it with *verlan* is very marked in *La Haine* and has confused academics in French-language departments (see *La Haine* & film criticism).

BEUR CINEMA

Documentary films and shorts made by Beur groups emerged in the late 1970s and by the mid 1980s several successful commercial features had appeared. These films have not been widely seen in Britain or the United States, but in France they provided a very different view of the culture of the 'second generation' to that offered by other sectors of French-speaking cinema. Beur cinema needs to be considered alongside the representations of the 'second generation' in films by mainstream French directors, 'first-generation' Maghreb film-makers and films made in North Africa. The 'first-generation' film-makers produced 'realist films or melodramas which show Arabs as the wretched, passive victims of French racism' (Tarr, 1993). Where does *La Haine* fit in this spectrum? Mathieu

'twenty per cent ... confessed to racist views'

Kassovitz must count as a mainstream French director in this context and, although there are some ways in which the depiction of Beur culture in *La Haine* may be more progressive than in mainstream cinema generally, Kassovitz has still been criticised by Beur film-makers like Karim Dridi (Tarr, 1997). (Beur cinema is discussed at greater length in Criticism later in this chapter.)

THE RACE AGENDA IN FRANCE

Immigration to France, mostly from North Africa, was curtailed in 1974 during the economic crisis which swept through Europe and North America, following the actions of the oil-exporting countries. Thereafter, a similar scenario to that in Britain during the 1980s saw the immigrant community blamed for unemployment by right-wing and openly racist politicians. Attempts to mobilise the large Beur community to resist racism were eventually eclipsed by the formation of the more broadly based SOS Racisme in 1984. But this was too late to halt the electoral successes of the Front National in the municipal elections of 1983. The Front has continued to capture local councils in south and south-west France (where many of the ex-settlers from Algeria now live) throughout the 1990s and to gain a national parliamentary presence. Since the legitimising of the Front National, the race attacks on black people in France have increased, as well as antagonism towards Beur culture and Islam (also the religion of former French colonies in sub-Saharan Africa). Frequent references to all Maghreb peoples as 'Arab' is a good example of a dismissal of distinct Arab and Berber cultures.

From a British or American perspective, it is very dangerous to play down racism at home in analysing racism in France, but there are significant differences, as set out by the *Guardian* columnist John Henley in December 1999: 'In a staggering recent survey, 20% of French people confessed to racist and xenophobic views of one kind or another – roughly twice the rate in comparable polls in Britain and Germany' (Henley, 1999). Henley argues that racism in France is insidious because it hides behind euphemisms such as those understood in *La Haine* – *quartier chaud* ('hot quarter') for an area with a high immigrant population or *banlieusards* ('suburbanites') to describe youths like Hubert and Saïd. At

the same time black people in France are excluded from certain forms
of employment:

> ... you could, for instance, count the number of black waiters in
> central Paris cafés on the finger of one well-manicured hand. Nor
> is there a black or North African newsreader to be seen on French
> television ... and despite the more than 2.5 million people *d'origine
> maghrebienne* with voting rights in France, try finding a North
> African MP in the National Assembly.
>
> *Henley, ibid.*

Although *La Haine* is not necessarily a film 'about racism', it is clearly
important in making visible the lives of people who have to survive in a
racist society and for this reason alone it stands as a political film.

ANTI-SEMITISM

Anti-Semitism has a long history in France, famously brought to
international attention with the Dreyfus trial at the end of the nineteenth
century. Many French Jews were sent to German concentration camps
with the collusion of the French Vichy administration between 1940
and 1944. Because of the 'myth' of resistance (i.e. the belief that most
French people had resisted the German Occupation), it has taken many
years since the liberation of France for the truth to emerge (i.e. most
people were relatively passive towards the Occupation and a significant
number were collaborators). Mathieu Kassovitz is very conscious of this
history. His father, Peter Kassovitz, fled Hungary in 1956, the son of a
concentration-camp survivor. In 1996 Mathieu Kassovitz played the lead
role in *Un héros tres discrèt*, a film which satirises the myth of resistance
and in 1999 he played a small role in his father's film, *Jakob the Liar*, based
on concentration-camp experiences.

One explanation of the scene in *La Haine*, in which the old man tells the
three youths the story about the train in Siberia and the trip to the labour
camp for Polish Jews, is that Kassovitz was attempting to remind his
audience that Jews had suffered too. He had considered and then rejected
playing the Vinz part himself, but he did play the skinhead who attacks Saïd
and Hubert, perhaps trying to 'objectify' his representation of Jewishness.

mistakes by the neighbourhood police

UNEMPLOYMENT

Youth unemployment in Western Europe has been rife since the mid 1970s. France has tended to experience a different business cycle from Britain and to adopt rather different measures to try to solve the problem. The results, however, are much the same, with youth unemployment representing a high percentage of overall unemployment. On the estates the situation is worse still. None of the youths in *La Haine* appears to be in work and the only example of support for education or training or even recreation is Hubert's gym – now burnt out. Petty crime and drug dealing are the only means of earning money. There was clearly a decision not to include the job centres etc. which feature in some Beur films.

THE POLICE IN FRANCE

France has three different police forces. The *gendarmerie* are national uniformed police responsible for security as an arm of the military. They don't appear in *La Haine*. The plainclothes police are the major problem in the film, in the form of 'Notre Dame', the officer in the American football jacket who shoots Vinz. They and the other uniformed police whom the youths meet are members of the Paris municipal force. The infamous 'CRS' are a separate force, the riot police in body armour with shields who chase the youths after Abdel's brother attacks the local police with a shotgun. The notoriety of the CRS developed after the student unrest of the late 1960s, but they are faceless figures of state power. Far more disturbing in the context of *La Haine* are the neighbourhood plainclothes police who have the power to make the youths' lives miserable on a daily basis.

The 'mistakes' by the neighbourhood police are such that police *bavures* (blunders) have become a generic feature of French films, including comedies. There have been over 300 'mortal blunders' – deaths in police custody/action since 1981 (see Vincendeau, 2000). Though many of these involve police racism, this is also indicative of a wider problem. Racism has been a specific problem in the police forces and, as in Britain and the US, a problem not automatically solved by recruiting black and Beur officers.

representations
in la haine

Representation is a slippery concept to grasp in relation to analysing a film, especially a film which appears to invite a direct reading of social conditions, as if it were indeed a window on a 'real world' of French youth in the mid 1990s. Like all films, *La Haine* is a construction – a text produced on the basis of a careful selection of certain visual and aural images, to the exclusion of others. Here we consider four representation issues: race, gender, the media and US v. French culture.

RACE

La Haine resists the assimilationist impulse of French culture in general by emphasising hybridity. It shares this approach with French rap music and some of the other French youth pictures, including Beur films. The references to 'difference' between the three youths are accepted as part of friendly banter. Saïd makes jokes about Vinz being a 'kike' and Hubert being 'chocolate'. In return Saïd is teased about his sister and mocked as a 'pseudo Arab'. These would be offensive comments made by anyone outside the accepted group, but it is similar to the use of the term 'nigger' between black youths and it has been argued that this kind of friendly insult strengthens the bonds between the youths and stresses the sense of unity through oppression.

The French estates do have more ethnic mixing than US housing projects and perhaps the black–*blanc*–Beur trio is not so outlandish. But this mixing only goes so far. The Vietnamese shopkeeper is identified as 'not one of us', and this could be read as another nod to American film models (where the Korean store owner is often the victim of shoplifting and portrayed as the enemy of the African-American community). This may be an instance of class solidarity – the shopkeeper is identified as an enemy, because of his ownership of the shop rather than his racial difference.

Racism is alluded to by Saïd when he says an Arab is never safe in a police station, and confirmed when he and Hubert are arrested and Vinz is not automatically assumed to be with them. But, despite this sequence, racism is much less evident in the film than might be expected from its setting. Indeed the most contentious issue – the Front National's definition of Islam as 'alien' – is not mentioned at all. Without some knowledge of the history of racist activity in France, British and American audiences could be forgiven for not totally understanding the sense of exclusion (the choice of the three youths as 'black–*blanc*–Beur' could be argued to be a metaphor about exclusion generally, rather than a reference to racial difference). There are coded references to specific instances of exclusion, as in the refusal of entry to the nightclub and the lack of meeting places for the youth on the estate. Black and Beur youth are forced on to the roof of an apartment block or into a basement. They are not allowed adult recreation but must sit in the children's play area, effectively kept as children by the authorities.

Some critics argue that Kassovitz ignores the specificities of the race agenda in France at the expense of importing American images of the 'hood' (see Alexander, 1995) or allowing Vinz to be the locus of hybridity, rather than Hubert or Saïd (Tarr, 1997). Conversely, David Styan, writing a companion piece to Karen Alexander's, is much more prepared to read the film as about the common identity of the three youths: 'What is relevant is that they are all stuck on the edge, lacking jobs and purpose. If they've any aim it is to resist categorisation and to forge a new French identity, both in spite and because of "those wearing leather jackets and voting Le Pen" whom they deride in the Metro' (Styan, 1995).

Other critics are similarly split, although the balance comes down on Kassovitz's side. What is unfortunate is that most of the Beur films, which might offer an alternative way of representing the lives of youths on the estates are not available for viewing in the UK.

GENDER

If *La Haine* is not about race, it is also not 'about' gender as such. It does not, for instance, explore how young men and young women react differently to conditions in *les banlieues*. It is a masculine story about three young men. There is no interest in the female characters other than as foils for the youths at particular moments. The sisters and mother/aunt/ grandmother provide the sense of a family needed to root the youths in

representations

The aggressive approach fails to work
with the two young women in the art gallery
– this is a production still: the framing
of the sequence is much tighter

the community, but not to offer a close relationship. The young women they meet in the art gallery are there only to emphasise the youths' exclusion, based on class and education/cultural knowledge.

La Haine has been criticised by feminist writers because of the generic references to other French films about similar issues, which also ignore women (i.e. most Beur films deal with young men – young Beur women are excluded from the discourse). More problematic still are the level of violence and the nihilism imported from American gang pictures. This is evident in so many ways: the violence of the language, the 'tough' clothes, the 'extreme' rap music, the aggressive gestures of Vinz, the sheer macho energy of the youths etc. (see Vincendeau, 2000).

Many 1990s' films depict the emasculation of male characters, shorn of any purpose, bewildered by what to do and resorting to sexist and violent behaviour and idle boasting of non-existent deeds in place of positive action. As David Styan points out, the youths in *La Haine* realise that their predicament is partly of their own making. When they riot they hurt themselves (burning down the school, wrecking Hubert's gym). The men who join the police are also caught in the trap and are 'every bit as insecure as the three protagonists; this is seen most clearly in the false bravado of the cop who has the final shot as *La Haine* itself crashes to the ground' (Styan, 1995). But the performances of the three leads work against this negative view of young men. By the time we get to the final shoot-out it is difficult to see the three youths as other than basically 'good lads' who could be redeemed. The real problem here is that our attention has been diverted to their behaviour – they, personally, could change – and away from the problems of society which have pushed them towards such behaviour.

THE MEDIA

Running throughout *La Haine* is a discourse about 'the media' (but represented largely by television and video). The film directly blames the media for the representations of *les banlieues* in the scene where the news crew approach Hubert, Vinz and Saïd at the children's play area. At other times, television is the omnipresent purveyor of 'news' about Abdel's condition and reinforcer of views about the riot. In Hubert's apartment, at

Saïd changes the poster to 'The World is Ours'

Darty's and on the video wall in the shopping centre, the youths watch the drama unfold. They are seen through the viewfinder of the news camera and the surveillance camera at Astérix's apartment. We see the police using video and the youths looking through the viewfinder of a stolen camera. In his next film *Assassins*, Kassovitz would attack the media head-on (and they retaliated by savaging him and the film).

US V. FRENCH CULTURE

Throughout this book there are numerous references to US cinema and US culture, but the emphasis in some of the critical writing on the importation of US youth culture is perhaps too great. No matter how much Mathieu Kassovitz has been influenced by US directors, no matter how positive he may feel have been some of the imports in helping to open up and 'hybridise' French culture, *La Haine* is still a French film set in a recognisable French location. A careful reading of the (British) subtitles and the general mise-en-scène shows that the American references are limited. The scenes in Paris at the art gallery and with the taxi and the attempted car theft might be an *hommage* to Scorsese (*After Hours*, US, 1985) but they are French scenes – imagine a US film about three youths, none of whom is confident to drive!

The cultural references are French cartoon characters, Smurfs (properly Belgian), Astérix and Obelix, and even two characters from Kassovitz's own childhood, Hercule and Pif. The music includes an American act but is largely French. The movie references to the *Lethal Weapon* series and to *Scarface* (US, 1983) (the poster which announces 'The World is Yours') are indeed American, but Saïd changes the poster to 'The World is Ours', and there are references to French films (possibly *Un monde sans pitié*, France, 1989 with the trick of the Eiffel tower lights).

Everything about the shooting of the film, the performances and the overall approach to the narrative denies Hollywood whilst validating American Independents. The success of *La Haine* is precisely in presenting US culture in a way that enhances rather than overwhelms its contribution to French debates. It presents itself as entertainment and social comment to both French and international audiences.

influences

Elsewhere in this book there are many references to films and film-making which seem to have influenced the making of *La Haine*. Some of these are assumptions by reviewers which say more about their own knowledge of cinema; others are derived from statements made by Mathieu Kassovitz himself. Kassovitz is not always a reliable source, but two comments which are repeated seem likely to be reliable indications of how he approached the film: *Mean Streets* is his favourite film and he was not consciously trying to create the French equivalent of a 'hood' film.

MEAN STREETS (US, 1973)

An important film in the establishment of the idea of 'American Independent Cinema', *Mean Streets* was Martin Scorsese's second commercial feature, following several films made in conjunction with his period at New York University film school, and *Box Car Bertha* (US, 1972), made for maverick independent producer Roger Corman. Although distributed by Warner Bros., *Mean Streets* was made independently with a low budget, using Corman's 'fast shooting' crew. It tells the story of a young man (Harvey Keitel), in New York's 'Little Italy', who is caught between pleasing his uncle, a mafia boss, an affair with his cousin Theresa, and a friendship with a wild young man (Robert de Niro). The action takes place largely at night in bars, backrooms, cars, the church and the cinema.

There are three obvious connections between *Mean Streets* and *La Haine* – the camerawork, the music and the relationship between the characters and their environment. With more control, slightly more money and much more experience than in his previous films, Scorsese was able to experiment with the camera. The results are memorable scenes, especially in the local bar in which Harvey Keitel makes an entrance to the Rolling Stones' 'Jumpin' Jack Flash' with the camera tracking back. The footage is manipulated by the use of slow motion and the bar is bathed in red. Scorsese himself refers back to Sam Fuller and his use of the tracking camera:

> Doing that one long take creates so much in emotional impact, giving you a sense of being swept up in the fury and the anger,

that you begin to understand more why it is happening. What Sam always says is that emotional violence is much more terrifying than physical violence.

quoted in Thompson & Christie, 1989

Here, surely, is the major influence on much of Kassovitz's camerawork. He may not have known about Fuller's work directly, although Fuller's camera style was noted by the *Cahiers* writers in the 1950s:

For many ambitious film directors, movements of the camera are dependent on dramatic composition. Never so for Fuller, in whose work they are, fortunately, totally gratuitous: it is in terms of the emotive power of the movement that the scene is organised.

Moullet, 1959

Whether it is from Scorsese or from his knowledge of American cinema gained via French criticism, Kassovitz was undoubtedly aware of the impact of his roving camera – to give a feeling of emotional attachment to the estate.

The music in *Mean Streets* has already been suggested as a model for *La Haine* (see Narrative & form) in terms of its mix of different forms, but the comparison can be extended to the use of specific tracks either to comment on the action or to confirm the 'authenticity' of a scene in terms of local culture (or subculture). *Mean Streets* was one of the first films to be remembered for its music, not as one or two memorable songs or melodies, but because the selection of different tracks 'fitted' the narrative. It was as if the authorial stamp of the director was evident in the choice of music as well as the direction of camera, lighting etc. All the music in *Mean Streets* is 'diegetic' – 'source music' as Scorsese calls it, playing on juke boxes, car radios etc. This is also the case in *La Haine*.

The setting and the characters in *Mean Streets* were close to Scorsese's own experience of growing up in Little Italy, and the actors, especially Harvey Keitel, were known to him through his NYU experience. There is a strong sense that these were not 'actors' playing roles, but local people being themselves. Although Kassovitz was not a resident of *les banlieues*, his close relationship with Koundé and Cassel and, through Cassel,

Taghmaoui, gives *La Haine* a similar sense of characters who 'belong' in their environment, and direction which knows how to organise the narrative around them.

If *Mean Streets* is a clear model for *La Haine* and Scorsese an iconic auteur figure, it is perhaps inevitable that there are direct references to other Scorsese films in *La Haine*: *Taxi Driver*, *Raging Bull* (US, 1980) (the camera roving around Hubert's boxing moves) and also possibly *After Hours* (see US v. French culture).

GANGSTERS & THE 'HOOD'

The relationship with *Mean Streets* is direct, but the overall relationship between Mathieu Kassovitz and US cinema is more complex. In the interviews which helped to promote the film, Kassovitz made two strong points: he didn't like Quentin Tarantino's work, he didn't want to be identified as a French Tarantino and he did not see *La Haine* as a 'hood' film.

The reluctance to be identified as a Gallic Tarantino is understandable, both because he needed to assert his individuality to promote the film, and because the comparison does not stand up. Tarantino, on evidence so far, seems much more concerned with genre and narrative tricks and much less concerned with any sense of 'political' purpose. The second issue is more interesting. The so-called 'hood' films constitute a generic hybrid, drawing on youth pictures and gang/gangster pictures made primarily by young African-American directors about life on the housing projects of major US cities. The most successful in critical and commercial terms was Jon Singleton's *Boyz 'N the Hood* (US, 1991), more a family melodrama set in South Central Los Angeles, and detailing the struggle by separated parents to prevent their son becoming yet another victim of the gun law, which kills so many young African-American males. Made by Singleton when he was just twenty-three and featuring an explicit political statement about the doleful future for young black men, the film created a major impact. There are clear parallels with *La Haine*, although in the latter it is the police rather than other youths who are the 'enemy' and the circulation of firearms is much more limited.

influences

Other films recognised as part of this cycle include *New Jack City*, a gangster film directed by Mario Van Peebles with a hero modelled on Al Pacino in *Scarface* (US, 1983) and *Juice* (US, 1992) directed by Ernest Dickerson, better known perhaps as cinematographer of Spike Lee's early films. *Juice* is closer to *La Haine* in its story of four youths involved in a shop robbery that goes wrong. These are films based on northern cities. *Menace II to Society* (US, 1993) from Allen and Albert Hughes and *South Central* (1992) by Steve Anderson are Los Angeles films closer to the melodrama of *Boyz 'N the Hood*. A further film, Dennis Hopper's *Colors* (US, 1988) covers Los Angeles (Hispanic) gangs partly from the perspective of two police officers. Finally there is *Hangin' With the Homeboys* (US, 1991) from Joseph Vasquez, which follows the adventures of a mixed group of African-American and Puerto Rican youths from the South Bronx in an alien Manhattan.

Kassovitz's comments reveal that he knew all about these films and admired them when he perceived them as 'independent' and 'committed', but that he feared the commercial exploitation of the cycle with which he didn't want to be associated.

AMERICAN AUTEURS

A director often mentioned by Kassovitz is Jim Jarmusch, one of the first directors of the new 'American Independent Cinema' in the 1980s to gain international recognition. *Stranger than Paradise* (US, 1984) won the 'best first feature' award at Cannes and was commercially successful (i.e. as a low-budget film its profit-to-cost ratio was high) in North America and around the world, including France. The leads, like those in *La Haine*, were three young men playing characters 'not unlike their everyday personalities' (Pierson, 1995).

If Kassovitz takes anything else from Jarmusch, it is perhaps the sense of a basic narrative drive that underpins a story that otherwise seems to meander along: 'Supposedly in Jarmusch's movies nothing happens, but you still get people escaping (*Down by Law* US, 1986)!' (Kassovitz, quoted in Bourguignon & Tobin, 1999). He also gets something from Jarmusch's contemporary, Spike Lee (like Martin Scorsese, Jarmusch and Lee were at

He quickly 'got into bed ...'

New York University Film School). Critics have pointed to the similarities in theme and storyline between Lee's *She's Gotta Have It* (US, 1986) and *Métisse* and between *La Haine* and *Do The Right Thing* (US, 1989) and *Clockers* (US, 1995).

Do The Right Thing is set in Lee's home territory of Bedford-Stuyvesant in New York during one blazing hot summer day when tension on the street is sparked into conflagration by the refusal of the Italian owner of a pizza parlour to put up images of heroes of African-American culture on the walls above his dining tables. *Clockers* is a 'hood'-style story about youths on an estate and drug dealing, with a concerned cop played by Harvey Keitel. Kassovitz is no doubt well versed in the sumptuous camerawork of Lee's earlier films, photographed by Ernest Dickerson, but it may be that Lee's attitude towards cinema has been more important than his aesthetics. Like Kassovitz, Lee has a father involved in the 'creative industries' (as a composer-musician). Lee is producer, writer and director of his films and also acts in them. Ten years older than Kassovitz, he made his first feature at twenty-eight and from the beginning ran his own production company, 40 Acres and a Mule (a name based on the [false] promise made to freed slaves after the Civil War). He quickly 'got into bed' with the Hollywood studios to make his films after *She's Gotta Have It*, whilst maintaining a high degree of control over the projects. Kassovitz is still working in France and Lee's role in developing his ideas about a commercially viable, but artistically independent African-American cinema make him a special case. But he offers a model of how to work successfully in the international film industry.

AMERICA OR FRANCE?

Mathieu Kassovitz rarely mentions French directors and French films in the interviews which helped promote *La Haine*. It is reasonable to assume that he has learned from the directors with whom he has worked as an actor, in particular his father, Peter, his business partner Luc Besson, and Jacques Audiard who gave him a leading role. But it would seem that although the cultural references are French, the visual style owes much to those graduates of NYU, Scorsese, Jarmusch and Lee and others who have shown supreme control of the camera and the edit suite (e.g. Stephen Spielberg in the earlier part of his career). 'Unlike many young French directors who are trained at FEMIS [a leading French film school], and who only swear by Godard, Pialat or Truffaut, Kassovitz readily quotes Scorsese and Spielberg' (a comment by Christophe D'Yvoire of *Studio* magazine, quoted in Vincendeau, 2000).

Kassovitz gets his cinephilia – his obsessive interest in cinema and especially auteur cinema – from his experience of French film culture, but his models do seem to be American:

> After the mistakes of my first film, I learned two things from watching the Coen brothers' films – you have to write exactly what you want to film, and then you have to film with a strong point of view. When you look at Orson Welles' films – he was a genius anyway – the point of view in his films is so strong that he can't be wrong.
>
> *Kassovitz, quoted by Loewenstein, 1995*

production & distribution

The budget for *La Haine* was around 15–16 million French francs (about £1.5 million or US$2.4 million). This is about the same as the budget for *Trainspotting* and slightly below the average for a French feature (considerably below the budget for a 'super production' like *The Horseman on the Roof* (France, 1995) which *La Haine* trounced at the box office.)

Mathieu Kassovitz was content with the budget, he had been used to much less on his previous films. It allowed him to prepare carefully for shooting on the estate. An idea of the nature of the shoot can be developed from the material in Narrative & form, and Style. Kassovitz became involved in the editing, sharing the work on Avid nonlinear suites, a relatively new development in France at the time.

The success of the film at Cannes a week before it opened in French cinemas signalled its great potential. The distributors, assuming a 'small' auteur film initially made only fifty prints available, but this was quickly raised to 250, more like the figure for a mainstream French or indeed American film release in France. *La Haine* played throughout the summer of 1995 and ended the year as number 13 at the French box office, with nearly 2 million admissions. This translates to a box office of around £8 million – puny by the standards of successful American blockbusters, but very good for a small film (like *Trainspotting* and *The Full Monty* (UK, 1997) it represents a very good profit-to-cost ratio). In Britain the film was released in November 1995 and for a foreign-language film it was remarkably successful, entering the Top 15 in *Screen International*'s chart and grossing a total of nearly £400,000. More significantly perhaps, *La Haine* has continued to be a cult film, screening on a regular basis at individual venues throughout the late 1990s. Its release in North America (where French-language films benefit from the substantial audience in French-speaking Canada), garnered a total box office of around US$500,000. The relatively disappointing American box office, behind several more conventional (i.e. relatively conservative) French films could be used to argue either that (a) the film was 'too French' for the American market or (b) that it was too American and not exotic enough. Either way, as in Britain, the film has gained a cult reputation in North America and has been heavily supported by users of the Internet Movie Database.

reception

La Haine has been termed a 'film event' in France (Jäckel, 1997). Throughout the summer it stimulated news stories, not least because it attracted a youth audience to the multiplex to see an auteur picture. Kassovitz himself had a lot to do with the fuss the film created. He plunged into the promotional round, but also initiated several unusual tie-ins. Gilles Favier, a documentary photographer who worked for the major news magazines, was commissioned to take photographs of the estates and their residents, which challenged the stereotypical view. These were published along with the scenario of the film. Some of these photographs were exhibited, along with stills from the film, at selected venues. Audiences were invited to take away copies of some of the photographs.

Writing and photography workshops for young people and youth workers were organised, some of which were run by Kassovitz and Favier (Elstob, 1997).

These actions helped to create forums to discuss the issues of the film. More discussion appeared on the internet with several fansites accompanying the official site for the film. The CD release of the original soundtrack was augmented by a second CD of songs 'inspired by the film' from rap artists invited to appear by Kassovitz. Two more bizarre outcomes of the film's release were an unsuccessful attempt by a French supermarket chain to cash in on the film's success by releasing a range of 'La Haine' clothing (Kassovitz refused permission) and a special screening of the film for the French Cabinet. This latter was intended to introduce the government to life on the estates. The right-wing government of Alain Juppé were reportedly not impressed by the film, but this episode is quite remarkable in the contemporary media world, and almost appears like a throwback to the 1960s, when politicians took 'youth icons' seriously as 'spokespersons'. Such was the impact of the film, which prompted coverage by many newspapers and started more discussion about the issue of *les banlieues*, fuelled no doubt by Kassovitz's provocative statements about the film being 'against the cops'. Sheila Johnston reports a nice rejoinder to this statement by a police official who refers to the film as 'a beautiful work of cinematographic art that can make us more aware of certain realities' (Johnston, 1995). As Johnston points out, it is difficult to imagine a similar comment by a British police official. It does show the potential for discussion of film culture in France and in that context we need to ask what the target youth audience made of the film.

The film certainly attracted some of the youths it purported to represent and some reports suggest that the strong language surprised and shocked young people themselves (Vincendeau, 2000). Significantly perhaps for some of the analyses of the film, there were suggestions that youth audiences recognised the major issue as class rather than race. However, some comments from audiences suggested that the character of Vinz was a problem. 'The Frenchman who pretends to be an Arab. He does not know who he is, he speaks *verlan*, he adopts the culture of the *cité*, but it does

'friends and families who died during its making'

not ring true. It is not a problem of race but of culture' (A youth quoted by Jäckel, 1997). This echoes comments made by some of the critics and by Jean-Louis Richet, the director of *L'états des lieux*, one of the films made from within the estate communities.

Anne Jäckel also reports that some audiences were confused by the film – they didn't understand why Vinz gave up the gun to Hubert, and some were completely baffled by the Russian story told by the old man. This isn't surprising: *La Haine* is an auteur film. It demands a different form of reading to that used for action-orientated films. The reference to history and its importance by Kassovitz reflects a growing sense by (generally older) film-makers and critics that young audiences have little sense of past events whether 'real' or cinematic. This is a charge often made, but difficult to prove or to evaluate if true, but what it does highlight is the ambition of *La Haine* in reaching out to different audiences and operating in both auteur and mainstream cinema contexts.

La Haine is dedicated to 'friends and families who died during its making'. It was based on a real incident and these incidents didn't stop after the film appeared. Press reports pointed to at least one riot in which youths may have been encouraged by the film to vent their anger after another incident. Screenings were made for the youths on the La Noë estate that featured in the film, and some youths visited a cinema complex for the first time. There were also reports of violence at screenings – a disturbing echo of the reports which suggested violent disturbances at screenings of *Boyz 'N the Hood* in Los Angeles (see Reader, 1995). Kassovitz maintained in all his interviews that he had no problems filming on the estate, but this was contradicted by several press reports. *La Haine* is a film that made an impact.

Perhaps the most important observation about the circulation and reception of *La Haine* is that interest in the film has been maintained. The failure of Kassovitz's follow-up, *Assassins*, dissipated interest to a certain extent, but a reasonable showing by his next feature which should appear in 2000 or 2001 will rekindle it.

criticism

Overall, *La Haine* received strong support, with the only negative comments in Britain and the US coming from reviewers who tended to compare the film unfavourably with Hollywood gangster or 'hood' films. For this very small minority the film was slow and its significance in terms of any form of political statement was either dismissed or ignored. (There were more dissenting voices in France, but again the majority view was very positive.)

The most detailed responses came from writers with an understanding of both Hollywood and European cinema and of French culture generally. French cinema benefits in coverage by Anglo-American academic writers in that it is a major interest not just for film or media studies academics, but also for those in modern-languages departments. The centrality of film within French culture means that aspects of French cinema are studied, in French, as part of degree courses in French language and culture. Academics concerned with this area of study are also able, as French speakers, to access film journals and internet sites written in French – often gaining access to materials denied to monolingual film studies academics and critics. In addition, because so much film theory derives originally from French philosophy and because the films of *la nouvelle vague* in the 1960s so influenced the early development of film studies, French cinema has remained an important subject for writing about cinema and, crucially, French films are more likely to gain a release in the UK and the US than films from most other non-English-speaking countries.

APPROACHES

Bérénice Reynaud offers a clear reading of *La Haine* and its importance by stressing the history of the Parisian authorities' attempt to push the poor out of the centre of the city (making Paris very different from London, for instance). She uses this to stress that the three youths in *La Haine* have an interracial friendship based on their common experience of 'social exclusion' – a term used here to distinguish the idea of shared experience of oppression from any sense that 'generational solidarity' supersedes issues of ethnic identity (as in a film like *Kids* (US, 1996)). Reynaud identifies *La Haine* as a film which helps to return French cinema to looking

'a place where nobody was born'

at the working class, this time in *les banlieues*. She identifies previous attempts during the Popular Front period in the 1930s and the more politicised films of the immediate post-1968 period. In particular, Reynaud refers to two of the films of the highest-profile 'political' director to be associated with the post-1968 period, Jean-Luc Godard. In *Deux ou trois choses que je sais d'elle* (*Two or three things I know about her* – France, 1967), '*elle*' is the Paris *banlieues* as well as the housewife/prostitute played by Marina Vlady. Godard mounts a scathing attack on the commercialisation of life in Paris and the prostitution of its values (i.e. forgetting the working classes who made it great). In his 1975 film, *Numéro Deux*, Godard returned to *les banlieues* as a location for an examination of the life of Sandrine, a refugee from North Africa, one of the working-class settlers forced to relocate after 1962. 'The *banlieue* started as a place where nobody was born. Now a generation later, the children of those who were forcibly pushed into these dormitory communities are telling their story with a vengeance' (Reynaud, 1996).

Reynaud's argument is that *La Haine* was successful because many people are worried about *les banlieues* – they expect them to explode in the near future and *La Haine* gives some insight into what is happening/might happen. The remainder of Reynaud's article is concerned with a discussion of *La Haine* in the context of the other '*banlieue* films' and television programmes which have finally brought into public discourse the issues of life for young people, in particular, 'the second generation'. These are often stories of *métissage* – 'an untranslatable term that literally means "inbreeding" but is used to convey a racial melting pot, something like 'multiculturalism' with a more populist, sensualist, almost physical flavour' (see comments about Kassovitz's first feature, *Métisse* in Background).

One feature of the 1990s' 'working-class films' is that many are set in France's second city, Marseilles, including Karim Dridi's *Bye Bye* (France, 1995), which some critics have placed ahead of *La Haine* as a film about the experience of 'the second generation'. Marseilles is both closer to North Africa and more working class in its profile. It is also closer to the areas of electoral success for the Front National. Reynaud sees *La Haine* as the most important of the films she discusses, picking out the scene in the public toilet and the youths' bewilderment at the old man's Siberian story as evidence of *La Haine*'s understanding that the oppression of *les banlieues* is rooted in a history. She makes the telling point that this reference to Vinz's 'community history' should be placed alongside colonial massacres in West Africa (graphically represented in Ousmane Sembene and Thierno Faty Sow's *Camp de Thiaroye* (Senegal, 1987)) and the systematic liquidisation of Maghrebians during the Algerian War. Her major criticism, levelled also at the other *banlieue* films, is the absence of narratives about women.

The only director from Reynaud's discussion whose work seems to be getting a release in the UK is Robert Gédiguian. Reynaud refers to his 1989 film *Dieu vomit les tièdes*. His 1997 film *Marius et Jeannette* was released in the UK and more recently *À la place du coeur* (France, 1998), which dealt with an interracial marriage between two teenagers who are persecuted by a racist police officer. Gédiguian makes films mostly about the working-class communities in Marseilles and has sometimes been likened to Ken Loach. Why his films rather than others have got a release is part of the mystery of distribution, but they do give British audiences some insight into a 'different' French cinema.

Ginette Vincendeau (2000) refers to *La Haine* as 'belonging to the new "genre" of youth-orientated and violent international neo-noir movies'. She makes the link to Scorsese and Tarantino and also to John Woo, citing the 'Mexican stand-off' at the end of the film. Her detailed analysis is mainly concerned with the representation of the social space of *les banlieues* and the 'authenticity' of Kassovitz's portrayal of its culture. She places *La Haine* in the context of other French films with similar concerns and discusses the contradiction between the American style of *La Haine*, with its appeal to an international youth culture, and the roots of the story in real events, further emphasised by realist traits such as documentary shooting. The rather chilling conclusion is that *La Haine* presents three young men who are detached from the long French tradition of working-class resistance and who belong instead to the new, international class of the excluded with its 'self-destructive, consumer-hungry, apolitical behaviour typical of international ghetto youth culture'.

Ginette Vincendau also appeared on a BBC radio programme which discussed *La Haine* in conjunction with *Trainspotting* (UK, 1996) and *Kids*.

'something meaningful to say'

Given the vagaries of distribution, these three films came out within six
months of each other in the UK, between November 1995 and May 1996.
The radio discussion took the three as examples of a new 'harder', 'tougher'
and 'more authentic' kind of youth-orientated cinema (although *Kids* was
generally not well received in the UK and the discussion suggested that the
film-maker had exploited his young actors). A totally separate analysis of
La Haine (Dixon, 1995) also linked the film to *Trainspotting*, but this time
on the basis that both films concerned the culture of housing estates. A
further link was then made to *Small Faces* (UK, 1995), Gilles McKinnon's
film about a group of youths on a 1960s' Glasgow housing estate. Dixon's
conclusions were that *La Haine* was far more successful than the two
British films, both in terms of its cinematic style and its representation of
lives on the estates.

Like several other commentators, Kevin Elstob comments on the use of
language in the film and for non-French speakers he offers an alternative
translation of one example of Saïd's tirades of invective:

'*Ça t'arracherait les poils du cul de dire bonjour?*' for example, is
scatalogically lyrical. It means something like, 'Would it kill you to say
hello?' However, such a flat translation undercuts a literal one: 'Would it
tear the hairs out of your ass to say hello?' (Elstob, 1997).

Susan Morrison considers *La Haine*, along with Wong Kar-wai's *Fallen
Angels* (Hong Kong, 1995), as one of 'Scorsese's children'. Writing after only
a single viewing of *La Haine*, but backed up by excellent research, she
teases out the Scorsese connection (see Contexts: Influences). Writing with
passion, Morrison conveys the excitement of a festival audience in Toronto
seeing *La Haine* for the first time, and she represents very well the way in
which the film appeals, beyond the issues it covers, to the sheer joy of great
film-making:

> ... Kassovitz's film shares with Scorsese's early work a power of
> method and economy of means put to use to tell an *histoire
> moralisé*. In these times when style and action seem to be all there
> is to most movies it's refreshing to find a film that not only has
> something meaningful to say, but says it in an innovative way.
>
> *Morrison, 1995*

bibliography

general film

Altman, Rick, *Film Genre*,
BFI, 1999
  Detailed exploration of the concept of
  film as genre

Bordwell, David, *Narration in the
Fiction Film*, Routledge, 1985
  A detailed study of narrative theory
  and structures

– – –, Staiger, Janet & Thompson,
Kristin, *The Classical Hollywood
Cinema: Film Style & Mode of
Production to 1960*, Routledge, 1985;
pbk 1995
  An authoritative study of cinema as
  institution, it covers film style and
  production

– – – & Thompson, Kristin, *Film Art*,
McGraw-Hill, 4th edn, 1993
  An introduction to film aesthetics for
  the non-specialist

Branson, Gill & Stafford, Roy, *The
Media Student's Book*, Routledge, 1999
(2nd edition)

Buckland, Warren, *Teach Yourself
Film Studies*, Hodder & Stoughton,
1998
  Very accessible, it gives an overview
  of key areas in film studies

Cook, Pam & Bernink, Mieke (eds),
The Cinema Book,
BFI, 1999 (2nd edition)

Corrigan, Tim, *A Short Guide To
Writing About Film*,
HarperCollins, 1994
  What it says: a practical guide for
  students

Dyer, Richard (with Paul McDonald),
Stars, BFI, 1998 (2nd edition)

A good introduction to the star
system

Easthope, Antony, *Classical Film
Theory*, Longman, 1993
  A clear overview of writing about
  film theory

Hayward, Susan, *Key Concepts in
Cinema Studies*,
Routledge, 1996

Hill, John & Gibson, Pamela Church
(eds), *The Oxford Guide to Film Studies*,
Oxford University Press, 1998
  Wide-ranging standard guide

Lapsley, Robert & Westlake, Michael,
Film Theory: An Introduction,
Manchester University Press, 1994

Maltby, Richard & Craven, Ian,
Hollywood Cinema,
Blackwell, 1995
  A comprehensive work on the
  Hollywood industry and its
  products

Nelmes, Jill (ed.),
Introduction to Film Studies,
Routledge, 1999 (2nd edition)
  Deals with several national
  cinemas and key concepts in film
  study

Nowell-Smith, Geoffrey (ed.),
The Oxford History of World Cinema,
Oxford University Press, 1996
  Hugely detailed and wide-
  ranging with many features on
  'stars'

Thomson, David, *A Biographical
Dictionary of the Cinema*,
Secker & Warburg, 1975
  Unashamedly driven by personal
  taste, but often stimulating

Turner, Graeme, *Film as Social Practice*, 3rd edn, Routledge, 1999
   Chapter four, 'Film Narrative', discusses structuralist theories of narrative

Wollen, Peter, *Signs and Meaning in the Cinema*,
BFI 1997 (revised new ed.)
   An important study in semiology
Readers should also explore the many relevant websites and journals.
Film Education and *Sight and Sound* are standard reading.

Valuable websites include:
The Internet Movie Database at
http://uk.imdb.com
Screensite at
http://www.tcf.ua.edu/screensite/contents.html
The Media and Communications Site at the University of Aberystwyth at
http://www.aber.ac.uk/~dgc/welcome.html
There are obviously many other university and studio websites which are worth exploring in relation to film studies.

la haine

Alexander, Karen, 'La Haine', *Vertigo*, vol. 1, no. 5, pp. 45–6, 1995

Astruc, Alexandre,
'The Birth of a New Avant-Garde: La Caméra-Stylo',
in Peter Graham (ed.), *The New Wave*, Secker & Warburg, 1948/1968

Austin, Guy, *An Introduction to Contemporary French Cinema*,
Manchester University Press, 1996
   An accessible account of some major trends in French cinema since the late 1960s

Bourguignon, Thomas & Tobin, Yann, 'Interview with Mathieu Kassovitz',
Projections 9,
Michel Ciment & Noël Herpe (eds),
Faber & Faber, 1999
   One of the most accessible articles on *La Haine*

Branston, Gill & Stafford, Roy,
The Media Student's Book, 2nd edn,
Routledge, 1999
   A useful background resource for

ideas about narrative, genre, production techniques etc.

Crofts, Stephen, 'Authorship and Hollywood',
in *The Oxford Guide to Film Studies*,
John Hill & Pamela Church Gibson (eds),
Oxford University Press, 1998

Dixon, Angus, Review of *La Haine*
posted on Glasgow University website,
1997

Elstob, Kevin, 'Review: La Haine',
in *Film Quarterly*, vol. 51 no. 2,
Winter 1997–8

Hayward, Susan *French National Cinema*, Routledge, 1993
   For French cinema generally, is good on contexts and historical perspective

Hayward, Susan & Vincendeau,
Ginette (eds),
French Film: Texts and Contexts,
2nd edn, Routledge, 2000

Henley, Jon, 'Clubland's true colours',
Guardian G2, 20 December 1999

la haine

Jäckel, Anne, *Paris banlieue – tour détour des jeunes,*
Education Department, Watershed Media Centre, Bristol, 1997

James, Barry, 'Assimilating in France',
New York Herald Tribune, 1 April, 1997

Johnson, Sheila,
Interview with Mathieu Kassovitz,
Independent, 19 October 1995

Loewenstein, Lael,
'Exploring the Dark Side', published on the website of UCLA (University of California, Los Angeles), 1995

McCabe, Bob, Interview with Mathieu Kassovitz,
Empire, November 1995

McNeill, Tony, 'Les banlieues' and 'La Haine',
lectures posted on the University of Sunderland website, 1998

Moullet, Luc, 'Sam Fuller: In Marlowe's Footsteps',
Cahiers du Cinéma 93, 1959; reprinted in Jim Hillier (ed.) *Cahiers du Cinéma: The 1950s,* Harvard University Press, 1985

Morrison, Susan, '*La Haine, Fallen Angels,* and Some Thoughts on Scorsese's Children',
CineAction no. 39, pp. 44–50, 1995

Pierson, John,
Spike, Mike, Slackers and Dykes,
Faber & Faber, 1995

Propp, Vladimir,
Morphology of the Folktale, University of Texas Press, 1968

Reader, Keith, 'After the Riot',
Sight & Sound, vol. 5, no. 11, pp. 12–14, November 1995

Reynaud, Berenice, 'le 'hood: *Hate and its neighbours',*
Film Comment, vol. 32, pp. 54–8, Mar-April 1996

Romney, Jonathan, 'La Haine',
Guardian, 17 November 1995, collected in *Short Orders,* Serpent's Tail, 1995

Salt, Barry, *Film Style & Technology: History & Analysis,*
Starword, 1992

Sarris, Andrew, 'Notes on the Auteur Theory in 1962',
in P. Adams Sitney (ed.), *Film Culture Reader,* Secker & Warburg, 1971

Shohat, Ella & Stam, Robert,
Unthinking Eurocentrism: Multiculturalism and the Media,
Routledge, 1994

Styan, David,
'So Far ... Everything is OK!',
Vertigo, vol. 1, no. 5, pp. 46–7, 1995

Tarr, Carrie, 'Questions of Identity in Beur Cinema: from *Tea in the Harem* to *Cheb'*,
Screen, vol. 34, no. 4, Winter 1993

– – – 'Ethnicity and Identity in *Métisse* and *La Haine* by Mathieu Kassovitz',
Multicultural France, Working Papers on Contemporary France, vol. 7, Tony Chafer (ed.), University of Portsmouth, 1997

Truffaut, François, 'Une certaine tendance du cinéma français',
Cahiers du cinéma 31, 1954

Vincendeau, Ginette (ed.),
Encyclopedia of European Cinema,
Cassell/British Film Institute, 1995

Vincendeau – Internet

– – – 'Designs on the *banlieue*: Mathieu Kassovitz's *La Haine* (1995)', in Hayward & Vincendeau (eds), op cit., 2000

Internet sources

Where possible specific references have been given for material found via internet searches. Web addresses have not been provided as they are liable to disappear during the lifetime of this book – several of those used for background have already gone. The Internet Movie Database is a useful starting point for a search, but a general search on major portals like Yahoo! or Alta Vista for "La Haine" or "Mathieu Kassovitz" (the quote marks are important in focusing the search) is still the best method. The fansite on Kassovitz run by Guillaume Colboc on http://kasso.citeweb.net/kasso/anglais/index1.htm is well worth a visit. Guillaume discovered Kassovitz when his school was used as a location for *Métisse*).

cinematic terms

American Independent Cinema a sector of US cinema formally recognised by the industry since the mid 1980s, with smaller budgets and slightly less conventional narratives than mainstream Hollywood. The term is now something of a misnomer since many 'Independent' films are financed by specialist divisions of major Hollywood studios

ASL average shot length

character functions an action associated with a character that has an important role in structuring a narrative. Vladimir Propp suggested that all fairy tales were structured using combinations of 31 character functions, such as 'the villain causes harm to a member of a family' – in *La Haine*, 'the police shoot Abdel'?

cinematography the art and science of capturing moving images. The cinematographer, in conjunction with the director, will make decisions about filmstock, lens, filters etc. This role is termed director of photography in the UK

diegesis/diegetic the world of the story, refers to components that are integral to the story

discourse taken from linguistics, this term suggests a regulated system of visual and verbal language with assumptions about what can be discussed on a certain topic. Thus a discourse on gender includes some ideas and excludes others

iconography derived from art history, the concept of a system of recurring signs (icons) across the films of a specific genre, such as the machine guns, cars and fashion items associated with gangster movies

identity in cultural studies the concept of how a sense of self is constructed (which may be at odds with assumptions about an individual held by others). Thus the development of a politics of identity

French cartoon characters cartoons and 'graphic novels' have more status in France than in the UK and possibly a more highbrow status than in the US. Astérix and Obelix, characters from Ancient Gaul who resist the Roman Empire, are national icons and the stars of recent French blockbusters. Hercule and Pif (replaced on American subtitles by Sylvester and Tweetie Pie) are cartoon characters in Communist comics going back to the 1950s (Vincendeau, 2000)

front office the management of a large media conglomerate which can make decisions affecting creative production without any direct contact with the film-making process

hegemony the power of one group over another, achieved through a successful struggle to persuade the subordinate group that the arrangements are in their interest – domination by consent

hybridity originally a term from biology relating to new organisms created by cross-breeding; now a concept describing any kind of 'mixed' entity which combines qualities from different parents. In cultural studies a crucial aspect of the contemporary world

cinematic terms

intertextuality the concept that media texts produce meanings through their relationship to other media texts, rather than directly through their relationship to reality

jump cut an editing transition between two shots which breaks the conventions of continuity editing, thus creating a jolting effect on the viewer

LS long shot

MCU medium close-up

MEDIA programme the major support programme to promote the audio-visual industry in Europe, funded by the European Union. Includes grants for training, script development (EURIMAGES) etc.

mise-en-scène originally a theatre term describing the staging of a scene and including lighting, costume, set design etc. Promoted as the basis for textual analysis of cinema by *Cahiers du cinéma* critics in the 1950s, the definition was later expanded to include camerawork. Some theorists believe the concept is less applicable to modern cinema

MLS medium long shot

montage loosely used to refer to film editing, montage has two specific meanings: the principle of juxtaposing images to create new meanings, introduced in Soviet cinema in the 1920s; the use of short sequences of related images, often 'library' stock, to give a quick impression of a particular event, industrial process etc. as used in Hollywood genre pictures of the studio period (1930–50)

MS medium shot

neo–noir 'noir' refers to the group of films made mostly in the 1940s in the US and Europe which were 'dark' both in theme and visual style. These films are now seen as a major influence on contemporary films with similar dark and 'tough' thematics, which, although usually shot in colour, have a similar visual style

non–diegetic not integral to the story

nouvelle vague the 'New Wave' of film-making in France in the late 1950s, associated with the young 'critics turned directors' of *Cahiers du cinéma*. The term New Wave has since been applied to many groups of film-makers who have challenged the prevailing modes of cinema

other a concept taken from work on the psychology of racism and colonialism. In order to justify the domination of one group over another, the subordinate group is seen as 'different', with qualities which are the negative of those of the dominant group. The dominant group needs to define 'otherness' to secure its own identity

picaresque a literary term, denoting the adventures of a likeable rogue, with a simple plot, episodic in structure, consisting of scenes of the hero's adventures

post genre although film-makers and audiences still recognise the characteristics of specific film genres, very few 'pure genre' films are still made. Most modern films are generic hybrids (see above) which use a mix of different genre characteristics. This is a 'post genre' cinema

cinematic terms

rough cut the first attempt to create a film with all the shots in sequence. The producers must decide at this stage if the original ideas about the narrative structure have worked out

signifier a term from semiotics – the study of signs. A signifier is an image or part of an image which is the code for a specific meaning (the 'signified').

Cinematic images often carry many signifiers, aural as well as visual

structuralism examines aspects of human society, including language, literature and social institutions, as integrated structures or systems in which parts only derive meaning and significance from their place within the system

credits

production company
Les Productions Lazennec, Le Studio Canal, La Sept Cinéma and Kasso Inc. Productions

director, writer
Mathieu Kassovitz

producers
Christophe Rossignon, Adeline Lecallier & Alain Rocca

cinematographer
Pierre Aïm

film editors
Mathieu Kassovitz & Scott Stevenson

sound/sound design
Vincent Tulli

assistant directors
Ludovic Bernard & Henri Pujol

runtime
UK, 95 mins

cast
Vinz – Vincent Cassel

Hubert – Hubert Koundé

Saïd – Saïd Taghmaoui

Samir – Karim Belkhadra

Darty – Edouard Montoute

Astérix – François Levantal

Santo – Solo

Inspector 'Notre Dame' – Marc Duret

Sarah – Heloise Rauth

Vinz's grandmother – Rywka Wajsbrot

Monsieur Toilettes – Tadek Lokcinski

Saïd's brother – Choukri Gabteni

Boy Blague – Nabil Ben Mhamed

Hubert's mother – Félicité Wouassi

Hubert's sister – Fatou Thioune

plain-clothes police – Zinedine Soualem

plain-clothes police – Bernie Bonvoisin

plain-clothes police – Cyril Ancelin

CRS Cave – Patrick Médioni

gallery girls – Julie Mauduech & Karin Viard

Benoît – Benoît Magimel

Médard – Médard Niang

Arash – Arash Mansour

young businessman – Abdel-Moulah Boujdouni

journalist – Mathilde Vitry

CRS TV journalist – Christian Moro

fat youth – JiBi

grocer – Thang-Long

DJ – Cut Killer

Saïd's sister – Sabrina Houicha

Vinz lookalike – Sandor Weitmann

gallery patron – Peter Kassovitz

Other titles in the series

Other titles available in the York Film Notes series:

Title	ISBN
8½ (Otto e mezzo)	0582 40488 6
A bout de souffle	0582 43182 4
Apocalypse Now	0582 43183 2
Battleship Potemkin	0582 40490 8
Blade Runner	0582 43198 0
Casablanca	0582 43200 6
Chinatown	0582 43199 9
Citizen Kane	0582 40493 2
Das Cabinet des Dr Caligari	0582 40494 0
Double Indemnity	0582 43196 4
Dracula	0582 43197 2
Easy Rider	0582 43195 6
Fargo	0582 43193 X
Fear Eats the Soul	0582 43224 3
Lawrence of Arabia	0582 43192 1
Psycho	0582 43191 3
Pulp Fiction	0582 40510 6
Romeo and Juliet	0582 43189 1
Some Like It Hot	0582 40503 3
Stagecoach	0582 43187 5
Taxi Driver	0582 40506 8
The Full Monty	0582 43181 6
The Godfather	0582 43188 3
The Piano	0582 43190 5
The Searchers	0582 40510 6
The Terminator	0582 43186 7
The Third Man	0582 40511 4
Thelma and Louise	0582 43184 0
Unforgiven	0582 43185 9

Also from York Notes

Also available in the **York Notes** range:

York Notes

The ultimate literature guies for GCSE students (or equivalent levels)

York Notes Advanced

Literature guies for A-level and undergraduate students (or equivalent levels)

York Personal Tutors

Personal tutoring on essential GCSE English and Maths topics

Available fro good bookshops.

For full details, please visit our website at www.longman-yorknotes.com